54

688

MINT

D1142346

Pictorial History of

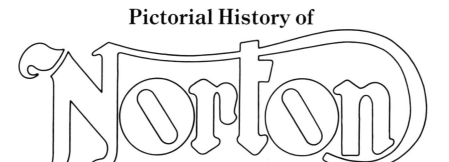

Norton

Motor Cycles

Jim Reynolds

TEMPLE PRESS

in association with

THE NATIONAL MOTORCYCLE MUSEUM

© Copyright Charles Herridge Ltd. 1985

First published 1985 by
Temple Press
an imprint of Newnes Books
84-88 The Centre
Feltham, Middlesex TW13 4BH
a division of
The Hamlyn Publishing Group Limited
and distributed for them by
The Hamlyn Publishing Group Limited
Rushden, Northants, England

Produced by Charles Herridge Ltd
Woodacott, Northam, Devon EX39 1NB

Designed by Bruce Aiken

Typeset by P&M Typesetting Ltd, Exeter

ISBN 0 600 35170 X

Printed in Great Britain by
Hazell Watson & Viney Limited,
Member of the BPCC Group,
Aylesbury, Bucks

Acknowledgements

In the course of research for this book it has been my pleasure to meet and correspond with many people who have been a great help, giving their time and knowledge freely. They include Freddie Frith, Doug Hele, Bob Collier, Syd Lucas, Michael Usher, Steve Lancefield, Bob Currie, Stephen Griffith, Titch Allen, John Hudson, John Stone, Chris East, Major Jenty Fairbank, Chaplain Porter and Percy Broad of the Salvation Army, Fred Hanks, Wally Flew, David Davies, and Jeff Clew.

Photographs in this book include some supplied by courtesy of The Imperial War Museum, East Midlands Allied Press, S R Keig Ltd, The Vintage Motor Cycle Club, and *Motor Cycle News*. Drawings by Martin Sayers and also by courtesy of Les Emery.

Jim Reynolds
1985

Dedication

To my wife, Valerie, without whose support I would never have taken the step of becoming a professional writer.
And to my sons, Iain and David, who both steadfastly refused to say "Norton" as their first word, despite my efforts.

Contents

Introduction

James Lansdowne Norton was born in Birmingham in 1869, the son of a cabinet maker. He was known locally as a bright boy with a high degree of mechanical skill, but those who gathered around the Norton home to wonder at the model steam engine the young Jimmy Norton had made could not have known that he was destined to give his name to a legend before his premature death, from heart disease, in 1925.

The model steam engine that astonished his neighbours was built when he was only ten years of age, and it was such an attraction that the local police asked him to take it out of the parlour window because the astonished onlookers were causing an obstruction. Such talent was not to be wasted, and when the time came to leave school, he was apprenticed to a toolmaker in Birmingham's jewellery quarter, where he learned to use his latent skill on the precision work that the jewellers demanded.

But James was not a healthy young man and one account of his youth tells of him travelling to America as a rest-cure after an illness; the date of that journey is the subject of some dispute, but it does seem that during that transatlantic voyage the young Norton was converted to the Salvationist belief, and soon after his return to Birmingham he became a member of the congregation at the Salvation Army's Birmingham Citadel. It was at the Citadel that he met Sarah Saxelby, whom he married as the 19th century drew to a close.

James and Sarah had five children, three sons and two daughters. The family lived in Sampson Road, close to the centre of Birmingham, and James was an active member of the congregation at the Salvation Army Citadel then thriving in the Sparkbrook area. His religious convictions were reflected in his business life, the machines bearing his name being noted for their solid build and reliability. He actually started the business of The Norton Manufacturing Company in 1898, in premises in Bradford Street, in the Digbeth area of Birmingham, and described himself as a "supplier of parts and fittings to the cycle trade". He had seen the cycle grow in popularity, and at one time was assembling complete machines, using boys from the Salvation Army to help with the work.

Amongst the contacts he made in the trade was Charles Garrard, the UK agent for the French Clement engines, who sold them to the growing number of small makers who were beginning to bolt small engines into cycle frames as the young motor cycle industry was growing. Garrard clearly had a healthy respect for Norton, referring customers in need of spares or service to the Norton company.

In 1902, James Norton began to make a complete motor cycle of his own, naturally using the Clement Garrard unit, and offering alternative types that included one of the very first ladies' models. In November 1902 *Motor Cycling* said: "That ladies are taking to motor cycling is now certain and amongst other firms, the Norton Manufacturing Company are making a special type of machine for the fair sex...." Such a novelty created a lot of interest, and in a letter to *The Scottish Cyclist and Motor Cyclist* in January 1914, Norton told how the first owner of a ladies' model had her portrait painted "practically life-size and it created quite a sensation at Derby".

Although he was a staunch advocate of light machines in his early days as a manufacturer, James Norton later developed larger machines, using French Peugeot engines. When this model was shown at an exhibition in the Bingley Halls, in Birmingham, he got into conversation with a young man who was to bring the Norton name a reputation for speed. H Rem Fowler was persuaded to buy one of the new V-twin models and enter it for the Auto Cycle Club's Tourist Trophy Race, to be held over a 15¾ mile course in the Isle of Man in 1907. James Norton travelled with Rem Fowler and acted as his pit attendant, and in later years Fowler recalled that the signals from Norton were limited to a waved reminder to keep pumping oil into the hard-working engine.

The race overall was won by Charles Collier, even then an experienced racing man on his Matchless, averaging 38.23mph for the ten laps. The twin cylinder class went to Fowler's Norton, at an average of 36.22mph, the Norton rider also setting the fastest lap at 42.91mph. Rem Fowler certainly did not have an easy ride, for apart from dealing with the unsurfaced roads of the time he had to replace a front inner tube after the original burst and brought him off at speed. He stopped to change plugs on six occasions and had another half-dozen stops for various adjustments. In these days of oil crises, it is worth noting that Rem Fowler's Norton averaged 87 miles to the gallon, the entrants in the twin-cylinder class being required to do at least 75mpg. The title Tourist Trophy races bore a direct relation to the origins of the machines taking part, and the fuel consumption regulation was deliberately designed to prevent freakish one-offs taking part. Later, the same machine took second place in a slow race organised by the Coventry Club, using the same gearing that it had for the Tourist Trophy Race – clearly not a highly tuned "special".

Later that year, at the Stanley Show in London – named after the touring cyclists' club that took its title from the famous explorer – Norton showed his new models, with his own design of engine. There was, of course, a V-twin very much like the TT winner, and there was a solid 82 x 120mm side-valve single called the Big 4. It was to remain in the range until 1954, a tribute to the James Norton philosophy of building machines to last. In 1911 the range was extended with another model that lasted in the catalogue for many years – the "3½" was intended to comply with the new restriction of TT entries to 500cc engine size, and its 79 x 100mm dimensions became synonymous with the Norton name. It was later titled the Model 16 and then 16H (H for Home Market) and under the latter title was to prove the mainstay of the Allied Forces despatch riders during the 1939–45 World War.

Those rugged but simple side-valve singles were the true foundations of the Norton name. The Big 4 performed as well as any of the V-twins of the era in private hands and the 500 became a major force as a record breaker at the Brooklands track and in the sprints and hill-climbs that were the most popular participant sport of the time. But James Norton, or "Pa" as he was more commonly known, was more concerned with making a good machine than with making a profit; he would even delay production while modifications that a weekend journey had proved desirable were made to machines being built up. He pushed himself hard to build and sell a decent, honest product; pushed too hard, in fact, and had to spend several months convalescing from a recurrence of the heart trouble, then came back to supervise a move from Floodgate Street to Sampson Road North. This attention to the product and not the profits had an inevitable result and in 1913 the Norton Manufacturing Company went into liquidation.

The company's assets – and they were very few, apart from the good name, for James Norton relied largely upon outside contractors to produce components which his modest workforce then assembled – were bought by R T Shelley Ltd, who had carried out machining work for Norton. James Norton and Mr Shelley became joint managing directors of Norton Motors Ltd, which in 1916 was moved to new premises in Phillips Street, Aston. The factory later expanded into the neighbouring road, which provided the address known to literally millions of motor cyclists the world over – Bracebridge Street.

It was from Bracebridge Street that James Norton's first overhead valve engine emerged in 1922, a lean and purposeful machine that lifted the world 500cc record for the flying start kilometre to 89.92mph. In 1923 the factory machines in the TT races were all ohv and the next year "Pa" Norton – by now a grey-haired man looking much older than his 55 years – realised a cherished ambition with another TT success. Two, in fact, with the Senior and Sidecar races going to his machines. The civic reception that the City of Birmingham gave him and his successful riders was James Norton's last public appearance; in April 1925 he succumbed to the illness that had dogged him for years. It was reported that he was working on a design for an aeroplane on his death-bed; he passed into legend as a man who filled every possible minute of his short life.

The company continued with Bill Mansell the major force in its direction. He had moved over from the Shelley company after the 1913 takeover and guided the company through a restructuring in 1926 that gave it a new title – Norton Motors (1926) Ltd – and led it on to become a major force in the world of motor cycling. After brief success with a new overhead camshaft machine in 1927, a redesign by Arthur Carroll gave the factory the basis of a model that was to dominate racing through the 1930s and again in the 1940s and early 1950s.

The whole history of the machines that bore James Norton's name is filled with the names of men who are in their own right part of motor cycling's story. It cannot have been just coincidence that drew them to the Norton marque, for many of them were hard-headed in their choice of machinery, and there was no lack of choice in the infant days of the motor cycle. From Rem Fowler through the likes of Bob McIntyre, they were probably drawn to a machine that was accepted as an honest attempt to give the customer the best possible value for money.

In the Beginning

Norton's reputation was built on a blend of racing success and road machines that were sturdy and reliable, even if at times they appeared to be a little staid. But the factory produced some outstanding examples of original thinking, including possibly the first ladies' model, as early as 1902, and Pa Norton's drawing for desmodromic valve operation before his death in 1925. There were outstanding men who carried the name in sporting areas, some of them from the factory, others just devoted to the sport of motor cycling and involved with Norton because that make best suited their purpose.

The experiments were many, the sportsmen even more numerous. Here are some of the outstanding examples that helped to further the Norton legend.

JAMES LANSDOWNE NORTON. James Lansdown Norton, photographed in 1925, shortly before his death from heart disease at the early age of 56. His prematurely aged appearance was one reason for him being known as "Pa" Norton, but the term was more a mark of respect from other makers, who appreciated his honest approach to making machines and his ability to think outside the conventional lines of the industry.

He drew up a layout for a desmodromic engine at one time, an idea that predated the Ducati development of the 1950s and showed just how far-seeing a man he was.

When he died, a fund was raised in his memory and contributions came from private enthusiasts and large companies alike. The fund was used to set up a scholarship in motor cycle engineering at Birmingham University.

THE ENERGETTE. James Norton's first motor cycle was the Energette, offered in a number of different forms, as this advertisement from November 1902 indicates. The reference to "Business, Touring or Racing" shows how wide the appeal of an economical motor cycle was thought to be in those very early days. The racing part was no idle boast, as *Motor Cycling* in May 1902 had reported on James Norton riding his Energette in a speed trial: "His time for two miles was 3 min. 37 secs. in the heat and the final was still faster, showing that a light motor bike (69lb) is capable of doing 33⅓ miles per hour."

Worthy of note is the address, The Garrard Depot, Bromsgrove Street, which was not a registered Norton address. It does indicate the high level of co-operation between Norton and Charles Garrard, who was his very first engine supplier.

CLEMENT GARRARD ENGINE. The Clement Garrard engine was 143cc, with an automatic inlet valve and side exhaust valve. The crankcase incorporated a mounting lug to bolt the unit to the front downtube of a cycle frame, with the cylinder barrel offset to the right to allow easy access and mounting of the inlet and exhaust systems.

This picture dates from 1903 and was heavily retouched for use as a publicity shot, with the brick background "whited out" to make the detail more clear. For the same reason, the driving belt has been left off the engine pulley, which was behind the flywheel.

THE ENERGETTE. The Energette's close relation to the pedal cycles of the era is clearly seen here. Fuel was carried in the front half of the large tank, with oil in the rear half, in which position James Norton claimed in an advertisement the risk of freezing was minimal.

The tank-top levers were for ignition advance and retard and the throttle, while a similar lever on the other side of the tank controlled the air/fuel mixture. Lubrication was a matter of operating the pump on the front left-hand side of the tank, which would pump oil into the crankcase. Operating the controls while riding the unmade roads of the early 1900s with no springing apart from the saddle springs was no easy task.

LIGHTWEIGHT MACHINES. During his earliest years as a manufacture, James Norton was a strong advocate of the lightweight machine. If the technical press suggested that the heavier machines were a better choice, he would buy advertising space in the same journal to contest the point. Here, in *The Motor Cycle* of August 8th, 1904, he makes it clear where his loyalties lie in the debate between heavy and light machines.

Norton followed this advertisement up with a detailed letter, published over two months later, telling how he had tried machines with weights from 70lb to 200lb and found the 99lb version "...the finest machine I have ridden." He went on to tell how three heavier machines had failed on a test hill, while "...a featherweight tourist machine, 60 x 70mm bore and stroke, outside flywheel, surmounted the hill without a stroke of the pedals."

1908 ENGINE. Norton's own design of side valve single set the standard for a solid and reliable engine that was to last as a basic design right through to the 1950s. New for the 1908 season was this 82 x 90mm engine, both its side valves operated mechanically by cams "of large size in order to give a rapid, and at the same time, smooth lift without shock, rockers being interposed between the cams and tappets."

An extension of the exhaust camshaft carried a sprocket, which drove the forward-mounted magneto by a chain enclosed in a "Norton" stamped case. Great emphasis was laid on the design of the valve chamber, which was separated from the cylinder wall by an air passage that aided cooling by removing one route of conducted heat from cylinder barrel to exhaust port. The port itself was designed to give a straight path for the exhaust gases, and combined with a straight pipe to prevent local overheating through unnecessary bends in the system.

1907 TT. Rem Fowler's success in the 1907 Tourist Trophy race brought Norton more fame, and ended his support of the lightweight motor cycle, even though he was to later design a two-stroke machine that never got into production.

Fowler's Peugeot-engined machine was long and low-built, a characteristic of the Norton design that stayed with the machines for many years. The long wheelbase helped handling on the indifferent surfaces of the day and permitted the machines to be built lower than the majority of other motor cycles, many of which still followed the bicycle style of the pioneers.

James Norton (right, with bow tie) was not a healthy man when this picture was taken before the 1907 TT race, having been away from the factory for four months during 1906 as a result of the heart trouble that dogged his adult life. After the race, Fowler was liberally covered with Manx dust and the acid solution the organisers had sprayed on the roads in an attempt to bind the surface and reduce the clouds of dust. A few days later his suit and gloves were full of holes!

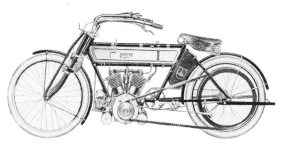

1908 TWIN. The 1908 season saw Norton's own twin cylinder engine introduced. It was very much like the Peugeot unit he had used in 1907, a 45 degree V-twin with automatic inlet valves and mechanical exhausts. It did not repeat its TT win of the previous year, Rem Fowler retiring when the valves stretched as he had no file with him to reduce the stem length. It was a simple matter of rushing into competition with a new engine that had not been properly developed.

The same engine was available for the 1909 season, and is shown here in that year's form, with an adjustable pulley gear that offered a range from 3.25 to 6:1 overall gearing. Norton was still mentioning the 1907 TT victory in his catalogue that year, but omitted any reference to the Peugeot engine. The machine was priced at 50 guineas.

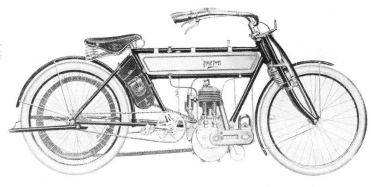

3½ SINGLE. Although he offered the V-twin, Norton was already concentrating his efforts on single cylinder machines by the end of 1908. This advertisement from December 1908 gives the price of the "3½" single as 40 guineas in the first year of the Norton-designed engine; it was to rise to 43 guineas the next year.

Although the sporting achievements listed here were all achieved on the Peugeot-engined twin, the only illustration is of the single, an early hint at the policy he was to follow.

1909 3½. For 1909, the "3½" Standard model used the 82 x 90mm engine in this 20 inch frame and had a simple stirrup type front brake that the catalogue described as "a special design of Norton Bowden". At the rear, a block operated on the inside of the belt rim, actuated from a forward-mounted pedal close to the engine driving pulley.

Already established, the livery was that which was to become so well known, the steel tank being enamelled, aluminised and lined in black and red.

The single already had a reputation for its reliable performance and Norton's catalogue was able to quote letters from as far as India that praised its ability to climb difficult hills. Nearer home, a Mr Harold Dean of Erdington, Birmingham, wrote to tell how his year-old machine had covered 3500 miles on journeys up to 70 miles "…and during the whole time has not caused me the slightest anxiety."

With the single proving popular and the Norton name well established, it looked as if James Norton was going to go from strength to strength. *The Cycle and Motor Cycle Trader* said of Norton in 1907: "The firm is one of the oldest in point of practical experience of motor bicycles in the United Kingdom." But the road ahead was not to be smooth.

Formative Years

REM FOWLER. Rem Fowler's 1907 Norton was acquired by Journalist John Griffith in the late 1950s and rebuilt. By then, the frame had been replaced by one of 1908 or 1909 pattern, the original having broken below the steering head early in its life. Rem was reunited with the machine at the National Motor Museum and it was put on display with the original telegram telling the factory of his win also on show. As Rem adopts a racing crouch of the period he is watched by (left to right) Alec Bennett, the 1924 Senior TT winner on a Norton, Bert Hopwood of Norton, Graham Walker and Lord Montagu of Beaulieu. This machine is now a star exhibit at the National Motorcycle Museum.

As the second decade of the century dawned, Norton concentrated on his single-cylinder models, but worked on alternatives. Notable amongst them was a two-stroke engine that never reached production.

The Big 4, with its long-stroke 82 x 120mm 633cc engine was proving to be an ideal sidecar machine, while the 79 x 100mm 490cc 16H was a high performance solo. But James Norton did not pay great attention to the basic matter of making a profit and in 1913 the company was taken over by R T Shelley; with the Shelley connection came Bob Shelley's brother-in-law, D R O'Donovan.

O'Donovan was a renowned tuner and his development of the 490cc engine at his Brooklands base soon produced the remarkable Brooklands Special (BS) which was sold with a certificate confirming that it had exceeded a speed of 75mph for a kilometre at Brooklands; or there was the Brooklands Road Special (BRS) version, which had attained 70mph. They can be accurately described as the first production racing machines.

BS TESTBED. The machine that O'Donovan used as a "slave" chassis to test all the BS and BRS engines at Brooklands stood in a corner of the works for many years, before being restored and finding a new home at the National Motor Museum in Beaulieu, Hampshire, thanks to Graham Walker who became the Museum's Curator after his retirement from the editorship of the weekly *Motor Cycling*. Graham, one of the finest motor cycling commentators ever, is seen here at the Brooklands Jubilee in July 1957, taking the grand old machine back to its former home.

1912 OLYMPIA SHOW. The 1912 range as shown at the Olympia Show had no revolutionary changes to offer, just detail changes as the singles continued to evolve, such as the larger tanks and "the larger spring filler caps" which were needed to make wayside refuelling more easy for unskilled garage assistants. But sporting success was a continuing feature of Norton's advertising.

The SUM Total

of

NORTON

SUCCESS IS EFFICIENCY !

Look out for the Un-approachable Norton, on

Stands Nos.

111 and 117,

Olympia,

and inspect the 1912 refinements. Larger tanks are fitted on the new models, and large spring filler caps.

Other detailed improvements make the Norton more than ever the machine for real hard work whilst the Norton "big four" is the passenger machine de luxe. Ample power, correct design, and efficiency down to the last detail.

SPEED—
May 21.—SHEFFIELD & HALLAMSHIRE M.C.C. ANNUAL RECORD ATTEMPT:
   Flying Kilometre, 3½ h.p. Norton (full touring machine), fastest time
   of the day, 70·39 miles per hour. (Officially timed by N.C.U.) ,
June 5.—SCARBOROUGH & DISTRICT M.C.C. SPEED TRIALS : 3½ h.p. Norton,
   fastest single-cylinder of the day, Gold Medal.

HILL-CLIMBING—
April 29.—BRISTOL B. & M.C. OPEN HILL CLIMB :
   Class for Touring Machines, 3½ h.p. Norton, Second on Formula.
   Class for Touring Machines (with fixed gear), 3½ h.p. Norton, First on
   Formula. 3½ h.p. Norton, fastest single cylinder of the day.
May 20.—SUTTON COLDFIELD A.C. MEMBERS' HILL CLIMB :
   Class 2, 3½ h.p. Norton, First.
June 10.—BIRMINGHAM M.C.C. OPEN HILL CLIMB, SHELSLEY WALSH :
   Class 2, 3½ h.p. Norton, First.
   Class 3, 3½ h.p. Norton, First.
June 18.—OXFORD UNIVERSITY M.C.C. HILL CLIMB :
   T.T. Norton, fastest time of the day.
   Class for T.T. Singles, 3½ h.p. Norton, First.
   Open Class, 3½ h.p. Norton, First.

RELIABILITY—
BIRMINGHAM—LAND'S END AND BACK :
   Three 3½ h.p. Nortons entered.   All three gained *full* marks.   Three
   Gold Medals.
SHEFFIELD—HOLYHEAD AND BACK :
   One 3½ h.p. Norton won the Hutton Shield and Special Prize.
BIRMINGHAM—LINCOLN AND BACK :
   3½ h.p. Norton won the Sangster Trophy.
BIRMINGHAM AND SUTTON RELIABILITY TRIAL :
   4½ h.p. Norton (big four) non-stop.   3½ h.p. Norton non-stop except
   for one puncture.

ECONOMY—
SCARBOROUGH M.C.C. PETROL CONSUMPTION TRIALS :
   3½ h.p. Norton, First.
SHEFFIELD & HALLAMSHIRE M.C.C. PETROL CONSUMPTION TRIALS :
   3½ h.p. Norton, ridden by a 14 stone rider, Second.
Mar. 18.—SOUTH AUSTRALIAN M.C.C. ADELAIDE PETROL CONSUMPTION TEST :
   3½ h.p. Norton, First.

FLEXIBILITY—
April 9.—WESTERN DISTRICT M.C.C. FLEXIBLE HILL CLIMB :
   3½ h.p. Norton, fastest time and slowest time, First for flexibility.

. . . **EFFICIENCY** . . .

S. & H.

Note the unique foot-boards giving perfectcomfort and grip. Note the position of toolbag, giving accessibility whilst riding. Note the neat and accessible engine, and the extreme " get-at-able-ness " of all parts. Note the very low seat, enabling you to plant both feet firmly on the ground. Note the handle-bar control and adjustable pulley.

Note the

Stand Nos.
111 and 117.

LIST FREE.

THE NORTON
Mfg. Co., Ltd.
Deritend Bridge,
Floodgate St.,
Birmingham.

THE UNAPPROACHABLE NORTON. By 1912 the 500cc engine was established as a 79 x 100mm unit and "The Unapproachable" was accepted as the Norton slogan – it was attributed to Rem Fowler, writing of his racing success.

The 79 x 100mm engine proved to be quite a lively performer, thanks to a fault in the early casting batches that resulted in the centre of the head sinking slightly and giving a higher compression ratio than standard. Dan Bradbury had one of these engines in his machine and made a name for himself in 1911 when he became the first man to officially exceed 70mph on a 500.

The tanktop toolbag was an early forerunner of the tank bags that are popular with today's touring riders. Forks were described as "special design of Norton Druid", a typical Norton habit of the time, possibly intended to disguise the fact that Nortons bought in so much of their machines from outside contractors.

FLYING MILE RECORD. Every record broken was announced to the buying public, to confirm the performance of the marque. When Percy Brewster set a new record for the flying-start mile at 73.57mph in July 1912, on a privately-owned 490, the accompanying picture cleverly showed the standard roadster model, to establish the close relationship between the roadster and the record breaker.

The London Agent at that time was Robertson's Motor Agency, of Great Portland Street. This was before the Shelley takeover, after which O'Donovan became the local agent, working from premises in Ridinghouse Street, between Great Portland Street and Regent Street.

No troubles to trace with C.A.V. Magnetos!

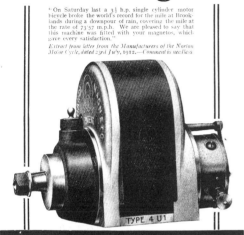
MAGNETOS. From early days, Norton was clever at getting component suppliers to mention his machines in their own advertisements. C A Vandervell supplied him with magnetos and were proud to mention the performance of his machines, as here in this 1913 page of Iliffe's *Tracing Troubles* booklet. Generous though C A V may have been in their mentions of Norton, he made no mention of their name in his catalogues, simply referring to the magnetos he used as "high tension".

The magneto was, in fact, very vulnerable to water and dirt thrown up by the front wheel, and the Severn Rubber Company offered a solution in a moulded casing that would fit over the instrument. It was priced at 2/6d.

MOTOR CYCLE OUTRIG. The touring rider was an obvious customer for the established rainwear makers and as early as 1913 Burberry's recognised the need for specially-designed clothing. As well as the British weather, riders had to cope with unmade roads that became quagmires when heavy rain fell. Any garment that protected the rider and allowed him to concentrate more on the task of coping with the road surface was a blessing and could command a good price from the thinking rider who could afford it. And it should be remembered that the motor cycle at this stage in its development was not the transport of the less well-off, but rather a means for the middle classes to either travel or seek sporting achievement; hence the interest of Messrs Burberry, with a "Motor Cycle Outrig" comprising coat, trousers and cap that cost a total of £6 – approximately one eighth the price of a Norton.

BROOKLANDS 1915. It was
natural that adverts in 1915
should have a patriotic slant, with
the First World War in progress.
At this stage in hostilities there
was no restriction on private
motoring and sporting events
carried on.

When a 490cc Norton beat
foreign machines up to 1000cc
capacity, it was a chance to
remind the public that the Norton
was an efficient British model.
The final phrase, "Be a TRUE
BRITON and keep your gold at
home", sums up the feelings of
the day, and Norton was not slow
to capitalise.

1914 TT. Works entries in the 1914
TT (seen in this damaged but
unique photograph) were fitted
with the optional Phillipson
expanding pulley on the
driveshaft and were ridden by the
Scottish Braid brothers, O G
(right) finishing 46th and brother
R J P 51st. The entry for the Senior
race that year was a record 111,
with 30 different manufacturers
represented. The Nortons may
have been helped over the
Mountain course with their
variable transmission, but were
no match for the Rudge Multi that
Cyril Pullin rode to win at a record
49.49mph.

SIDECAR RECORD. While the
Big 4 was the sidecar machine of
the range, records in the sidecar
class were attacked with the
proven 490cc engine. It was so
fast by the standards of 1915 that a
bigger capacity engine was not
necessary, as this advertisement
from September 1915 shows. The
riding and tuning skills of
O'Donovan were at work again,
taking records in 500, 750 and
1000cc classes, which gave
another opportunity to remind
buyers that they should Buy
British.

The country may have been at
war, but Bartletts of Kilburn
seemed to be prospering, with
new showrooms in Great
Portland Street to show the
Norton machines as O'Donovan
concentrated on the work of
tuning.

World's 500 c.c. Record Regained

Last week we learned our long-standing kilo record of 81'05 had been broken in Switzerland with a speed of 81'5, upon which we congratulate the rider and also maker of machine. In spite of the fearful track conditions at Brooklands, Mr. O'Donovan took down an **ABSOLUTELY STANDARD ENGINE** and considerably exceeded the Swiss speed, made on a smooth, straight road, apparently with a following wind. The **NORTON SPEED** was

82·85

This, remember, on a pot-holey, undulating surface with a cross wind, it proves the 490 c.c. **NORTON STILL UNAPPROACHABLE** for efficiency, power and speed.

Mr. O. R. O'DONOVAN and his T.T. NORTON.

LONDON:
BARTLETT & CO., The Parade, Kilburn.

NORTON WORKS,
BIRMINGHAM.

500cc RECORD. The 490cc engine became a regular record breaker in O'Donovan's skilled hands, and the man himself became a personality of some note – although he was not renowned as an approachable type.

His success in June 1915, reaching a speed of 82.85mph, naturally made for an eye-catching advertisement. But no mention was made of his showroom, the company diplomatically mentioning only Bartlett of Kilburn, whose premises were then some miles away from O'Donovan's London address.

BIG FOUR. The 1916 range included the racing options on the Tourist Trophy 490cc model, even though the country had been at war for two years. But prices were beginning to rise, with materials in short supply, and the Big 4 Combination had gone from its 1915 price of £80 to £85.

The company was now in its Aston Brook Street premises, right next to Shelley's works, and from there it was in time to expand and take on more space that gave it frontage onto Bracebridge Street. Meanwhile, the new works was busy on munitions work and supplying the Big 4 model – in belt drive form – to the Russian Army.

SIDECARS. It was natural for 'Pa' Norton to offer sidecars in the range, since he was a staunch supporter of them as family transport. Chassis were built up in the Norton factory and the bodies "bought in" from the Watsonian Sidecar Company. The Big 4 model was made with sidecar lugs as standard and could be ordered with all-chain transmission and a Sturmey-Archer three-speed gearbox, a cush drive being built into the rear hub. During the development of the gearbox, Sturmey Archer used three Big 4's as test machines, one of them covering 32,000 miles during tests.

An improved Norton chassis.

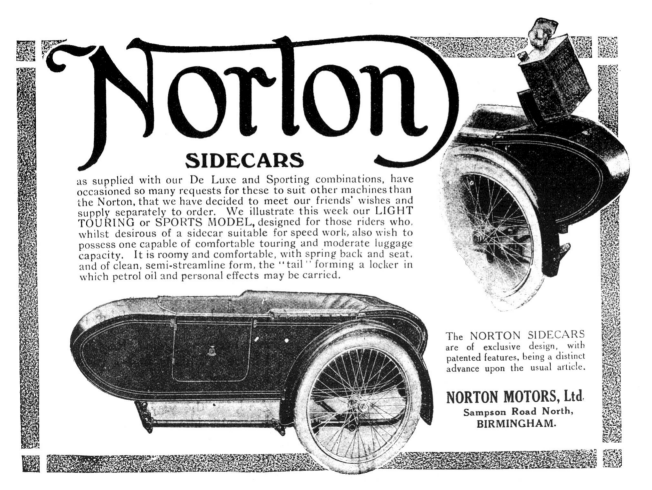

Norton
SIDECARS

as supplied with our De Luxe and Sporting combinations, have occasioned so many requests for these to suit other machines than the Norton, that we have decided to meet our friends' wishes and supply separately to order. We illustrate this week our LIGHT TOURING or SPORTS MODEL, designed for those riders who, whilst desirous of a sidecar suitable for speed work, also wish to possess one capable of comfortable touring and moderate luggage capacity. It is roomy and comfortable, with spring back and seat, and of clean, semi-streamline form, the "tail" forming a locker in which petrol oil and personal effects may be carried.

The NORTON SIDECARS are of exclusive design, with patented features, being a distinct advance upon the usual article.

NORTON MOTORS, Ltd.
Sampson Road North,
BIRMINGHAM.

1916 SIDECAR CHASSIS. In 1916 a simplified sidecar chassis was introduced. The front rail of the chassis incorporated spring mounting points instead of the earlier method of a separate mounting tube above the basic chassis. At the rear, the body was suspended on C-springs, attached to the chassis rails by U-bolts.

Each tube in the new chassis was straight, apart from that attaching to the chain stay, and was shorter than its predecessor. The result was a weight saving of 7lb.

GEARING TIPS. D R O'Donovan's hints and tips for tuning the racing BS and BRS engines included suitable gear ratios. For belt-driven models, 3.7:1 was recommended for maximum speed "provided a flying start of at least ¼ mile is obtainable." For hill-climbs, such as the Style Cop venue near Rugeley, Staffordshire, he recommended going down to 4.75 or even 5:1, while the chain-driven models should use "a ratio giving from ½ to ¾ lower than that which is suitable with belt drive."

OLD MIRACLE. O'Donovan's slave rolling chassis was rebuilt as a complete machine to become known as "Old Miracle". It is still a regular competitor in the annual Pioneer Run from London to Brighton, loaned by the National Motor Museum to a variety of riders. Here, the late Peter Arnold looks suitably pleased at having reached the Brighton seafront despite the problems that direct drive and single gear presented in the traffic of 1957. Its easy, loping gait and the difficulties that stopping pose combine to make it a regular early finisher in the Run, but do demand a high degree of riding skill.

A Reputation for Solidity

Norton entered the 1920s with a reputation for machines that were well established before the Great War, but their sporting success was largely achieved at Brooklands, the faithful O'Donovan having opened his postwar account with 14 new sidecar records. As usual he used a 490cc model, in this instance fitted with a Canoelet sidecar, to set new figures for the 500, 750 and 1000cc classes, the longest the 3 hours at 50.92mph.

But the Tourist Trophy races saw the famous 490 Norton beaten into second place, and even if the winning margin was only 3 minutes 52 seconds, people tend to remember winners and not runners-up. In 1921, a team of five works entries in the coveted Senior TT could only produce a best performance of sixth place, the race going to Howard Davies' remarkable little overhead valve 350 AJS. Clearly, Norton needed something new if they were to keep their sporting reputation, and the ohv design that James Norton had drawn as long ago as 1913 was dusted off and given a second look. It was to prove a major step forward when the new model was sorted out, and by the end of the decade they took even greater steps forward, as we shall see.

Meanwhile, James Norton made a journey around South Africa, using one of his favourite Big 4 sidecar outfits. He reported that there were opportunities for manufacturers to sell machines to that market, even though the Americans were already established there. It was typical of the founder of the firm that he went to see for himself what was needed, even though he was not strong physically.

1920 16H. Victor Horsman caught TT fever when he watched the very first races in 1907. He rode in the races on a Norton 16H in 1920 and, 21, but did not figure in the results. His adoption of full racing leathers for the 1920 event was not a matter of meeting the regulations, for two years later the winner of one race wore a cricket jumper and horse riding breeches.

Victor went on to become a leading light at Brooklands before setting up in business in Liverpool, the Norton agency being one of several he held.

1921 MAINTENANCE INSTRUCTIONS. The factory sensibly recognised that the private owner would not always have all the recommended tools to hand for an overhaul. The 1921 Maintenance Instructions booklet showed this handy method of removing the engine sprocket, but added "this should never be resorted to unless a proper sprocket-drawer is not procurable." The tommy-bar was placed over the keyway behind the sprocket and given a sharp blow, to loosen the key. If this did not loosen the sprocket enough, the tommy-bar could then be placed on a tooth of the sprocket and tapped again, to loosen the sprocket on the tapered mainshaft.

1921 BIG FOUR. The 1921 range was headed by the Big Four, with all-chain drive now standardised. The tanktop tool bag had gone, but chains were enclosed in pressed steel oilbaths and road dirt was kept off the front-mounted magneto by deep valances on the front mudguard. The dropped-tube frame was now used throughout the range and allowed a more substantial mounting of the saddle, the springs bolting directly onto the upper chainstays.

The Big 4 was priced at £120, with a Lucas Magdyno lighting set available as an extra at £21. A bulb horn was £1.7.6d or an electric horn £2.12.6d.

1921 16H. The 16H title entered the catalogue, describing the 79 x 100mm single that the factory claimed was "...undoubtedly the fastest countershaft-geared 3½hp machine extant." Standard gear ratios were 4½, 7½ and 12:1, with an optional close ratio box available giving 4½, 5¼ and 7½ gearing. In the latter case, a kickstart was available only to special order.

The 16H cost £115, with the 70mph BRS engine an extra £12 and the 75mph BS version an extra £22, which included a Binks' Rat-trap and standard B & B carburettors.

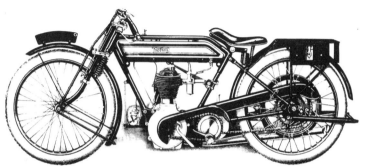

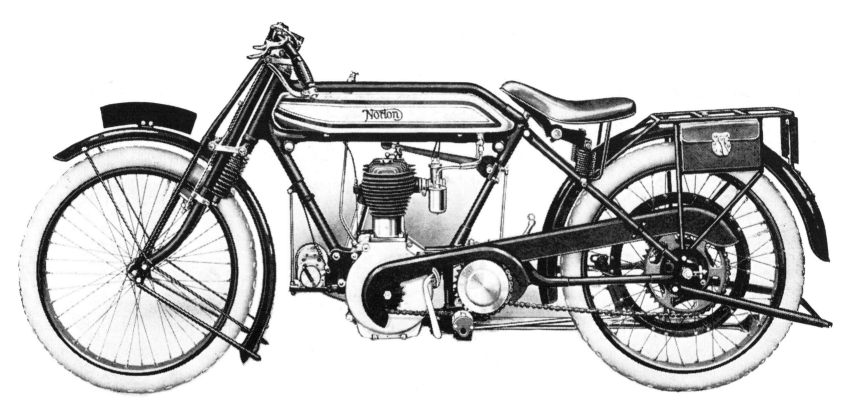

1921 17C COLONIAL. Priced at £117 was the 17C 3½hp Colonial model, with a ground clearance two inches higher than the four inches of the 16H home market version. The tank held two gallons (16H 1¾ gallons) and the standard gear ratios were 4½, 7¾ and 13¼ to 1.

Although the 17C was intended for Colonial use, the BS and BRS engines were available.

BELT DRIVE 9TT. Belt drive lived on with the 9TT model, an adjustable pulley offering ratios from 6 to 4:1. The weight was 203lb and the wheelbase 52½ inches. At £80 it was a true production racing model, with the BS and BRS engines available at extra cost. It was the only model in the 1921 range shown without sidecar lugs as a standard feature of the frame.

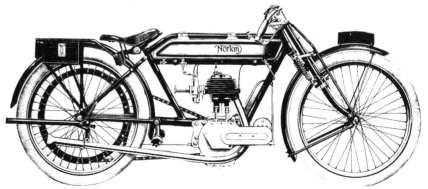

FAMILY SIDECAR. For the family man, the Family sidecar, with a dickey seat that also doubled as a luggage compartment. Naturally, it was shown with the Big 4 model.

Priced at £34, the Family sidecar could be fitted with the Triplex screen and dash cover as shown here, at an extra £4.10.0d.

SPORTING SIDECAR. With O'Donovan breaking sidecar records, it was natural that the factory should offer a sporting chair to go with the tuned versions of the 16H or 17C. The Light Sporting model could be used for racing or touring, the backrest being adjustable to allow the passenger to tuck himself out of the breeze if it was a day for racing. The simple, slim body with no luggage accommodation allowed a more modest price of £24.10.0d.

1923 SIDECAR TT. George Tucker from Bristol won the 1924 Sidecar TT having finished third in the 1923 race, on a 588cc model on each occasion. Here he is before the 1923 event, looking very relaxed – TT winners of the early 1920s were very weary when the race was over! The supplementary fuel tank seen here was fitted for the 3-lap race, but in 1924 the 4-lap race meant a pit stop was necessary. The Hughes sidecar was regarded as the ultimate sporting chair of the day.

DELIVERY OUTFIT. For 1922, the sidecar range was supplemented with a commercial box, which could be swapped with one of the passenger bodies on the same chassis. The inside of the box measured 51 inches x 19 wide x 18 deep yet the whole outfit was only 54 inches wide.

Times were getting hard, and money was not so easy. The commercial box cost £18, and the catalogue offered deferred payments of £4.10.0d deposit and 12 monthly payments of £1.5.0d. The Lucas Magdyno lighting set was now available at a cost of £11.12.6d which was a considerable reduction on the 1921 catalogue price of £21.

MAUDES TROPHY. The Maudes Trophy, presented by Maudes Motor Mart of Exeter, was first presented in 1923, for the most meritorious performance by a manufacturer during the year. In September, J D Pope of the ACU selected standard parts from the factory stores and a Model 18 engine was assembled. Fitted into a frame by O'Donovan, it was run-in for 29 laps of Brooklands, then locked away.

The next day a team of (left to right) Nigel Spring, D R O'Donovan and Bert Denly shared the ride to break records from the 7 hours to 12 hours, averaging some 64mph. The Maudes Trophy went to Bracebridge Street.

1927 FORKS. Forks being the part that most frequently needed attention after an accident, they could be ordered as a complete assembly or in separate components. 2298 was described as a Norton-Druid type, suitable for the 16H and No 2 models, 2318 was the Norton-Webb for the Model 18 and several others, while the 2352 was termed the Norton-Druid Mk 2, and was fitted to the 17C Colonial 490cc side valver.

TT TROPHIES. What a proud moment for Pa Norton, standing between the Senior and Sidecar Tourist Trophies at a Civic Reception in Birmingham in July 1924. Looking over his shoulder is Walter Moore, who developed the Norton ohv design into a race winner and was a team manager who believed in personal involvement, passengering George Tucker in his TT winning ride.

This was Pa Norton's last public appearance; within a year he succumbed to the heart disease that had affected him for years. The trade mourned the passing of one of its most influential pioneers.

1927 FRAMES. This page from the 1927 Parts Catalogue shows the range of frames available from the works. 2290 was for the 17C Colonial version of the side valve, 2291 the lower ground clearance 16H, 2292 shows the bent lower top rail to accommodate the ohv engine of the Model 18, as do 2293 (Model 19) and 2295 (Model 24). 2294 was for the Model 14. Prices ranged from £11 to £13.

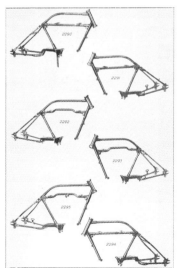

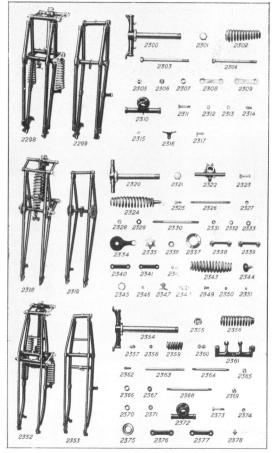

VALVE SPRING CHANGE. The overhead valve engine as a type was regarded with suspicion by riders who were used to changing valve springs at the roadside, an easy task with a side valve engine, but a problem with the newer type. This ingenious tool made spring changing possible without removing the cylinder head, one U-shaped bar secured in a threaded sleeve being inserted through the normal plug hole and tightened with the rod against the valve head, thus keeping it in place while the compressing tool was screwed into the other threaded hole in the head to compress the spring as the retaining collets were removed and the spring changed.

1926 MODEL 18. A lovely 1926 Model 18 with Hughes sidecar still giving enjoyment 34 years after it was made. Frank Farrington is well known in Vintage MCC circles and here he and passenger John Bone make their way to a First Class award in the 1960 Banbury Run. The machine is fitted with the 8 inch front brake and had been raced in the 1920s; the engine was modified by the Lancashire sprinter H F Brockbank.

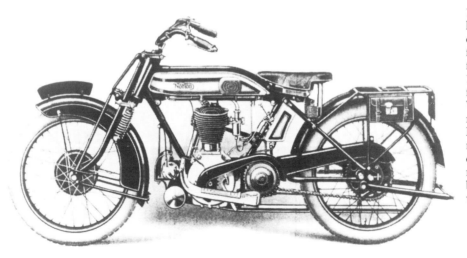

1927 BIG 4. The Big 4 of 1927 was looking very dated and if belt drive replaced the chain and the front drum brake was swapped for the stirrup brake of the early 1920s, it might easily be mistaken for a veteran of pre-First World War days. Its inclusion in the range was a throwback to Pa Norton's great affection for the model, but fashion was moving on and something fresh was needed to persuade the average buyer that Norton's biggest model was worthy of his consideration.

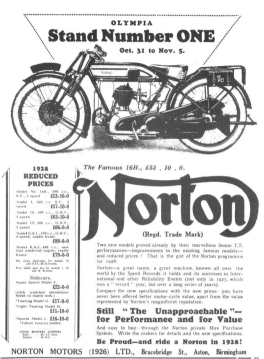

CS1 RACING DEBUT. In 1925 Dougal Marchant set a new flying kilometre record for 350s at over 100mph on an overhead camshaft Chater Lea – Blackburne, and Alec Bennett rode the new ohc 350cc Velocette to win the Junior TT in 1926. These were clear signs that the pushrod Norton was dated as a racing machine, so Walter Moore produced a design for a 79 x 100mm ohc engine (what other dimension would he have dared suggest to Norton?) in his own time, then persuaded Norton to build it.

In the 1927 Senior the Walter Moore camshaft design proved its point. Stanley Woods was leading by four minutes, but was not told this when he stopped for fuel and carried on at the same speed until the clutch failed and he retired. Alec Bennett, a shrewd judge of a winning machine, paced himself to win at an average of 68.4mph. Here he takes a little refreshment after this historic victory as Bill Mansell behind the machine looks suitably pleased at the new CS1 model's racing debut.

1927 16H. The success of the new CS1 model in the TT was mentioned in the company's advertisements, but reduced prices hinted at hard times as the company tightened its belt to get through the period of the Depression.

The faithful 16H was the featured machine, its price at £53.10.0d still noticeably higher than equivalent models from other major makers, such as Triumph's 500cc N De Luxe side valver. The lines of the exhaust pipe slavishly followed the fashion set by the CS1 and its left-hand exhaust port, and bending the 16H pipe around the bottom of the front down tube to pass it back along the left of the machine must have been a time-consuming job compared with the simpler style of earlier models. It is worth noting that a Lucas Magdyno lighting set for a solo was priced at £5.15.0d compared with the 1921 figure of £21. Times were hard indeed!

1928 MODEL 18. The 1928 Model 18 was priced at £63.10.0d and could be supplied with dry sump lubrication at an extra £3.10.0d with Walter Moore-designed oil pump as fitted to the CS1. The pushrod and side valve models used the diamond frame with twin chain stays, apart from the sporting ES2 (priced at £79) which shared with the CS1 the cradle frame with an extra stay from above the gearbox to the spindle lug. This machine has a later front fork and wheel fitted.

DOUBLE-BARRELLED SILENCER. The double-barrelled silencer was introduced for the 1928 season, using cast alloy ends and steel tubing for the body. The tailpipe was available black or plated.

The impressive alloy primary chaincase would not be polished like this as standard, nor would the crankcases and the magneto shield. But a customer could order special polishing if he preferred and was prepared to pay a little extra.

1929 CS1. The CS1 engine gave some 28bhp at 5500rpm on a compression ratio of 7:1. The overhead camshaft was driven by bevels and a vertical shaft with splined couplings. The Lucas magneto drive was by chain from a double engine sprocket, which gave the timing side of the engine a very clean, uncluttered appearance.

A Sturmey Archer three-speed gearbox with non-positive stop foot change was standard and 8 inch brakes front and rear were part of the Enfield wheels that carried the 57¾ inches wheelbase cradle frame. The CS1 designation simply stood for "Camshaft 1".

SADDLE TANK. For 1929 saddle tanks replaced the traditional flat tanks that had been in common use before – the CS1 had used the more modern style from its introduction and what worked on the racing models could be accepted on humble roadsters. Even the 16H was altered and one is shown here in a factory picture of that year. It was held by four bolts through frame lugs, and was insulated from vibration by rubber top-hat section buffers with the smaller section passing down into the lug.

1929 MODEL 18. Fully equipped for touring, a Model 18 was a long-legged and flexible machine that would take the hills in its stride, and the 1929 double chainstay rigid frame gave security on metalled roads. The standard carburetter was a 1 inch Brown and Barlow, but for the faster rider an Amal with a 1¹⁄₁₆ inch choke size was available. The phrase "When God made the hills, he made them for Nortons" aptly summed up its top-gear performance; it was capable of an honest 75mph without strain, yet could return over 100 miles to a gallon of fuel.

1929 SPANISH GRAND PRIX. The final racing success of the 1920s came in the Spanish Grand Prix – given the European Grand Prix title in 1929 – with new team member Tim Hunt winning the 500cc class and Dennis Mansell the 600cc Sidecar race. It was the beginning of Joe Craig's management of the team, which explains him looking almost as happy as the winner himself! On the left is Stanley Woods, who retired on this occasion.

Walter Moore left Norton to join the German NSU factory at the end of 1929, for a rumoured £5500 per annum plus "fringe benefits", taking with him the drawings for the CS1 engine as it had been produced in his own spare time and was therefore a Moore design, not a Norton. His place was taken by Arthur Carroll, whose brief to design a better engine was no doubt spurred on by Alec Bennett's refusal to ride a Norton in the 1929 Senior TT, he reportedly telling the directors that their machine had no chance of winning; he proved his point by finishing second to Charlie Dodson's Sunbeam – on another Sunbeam.

As the 1930s approached, the Norton range was looking rather dated, with its long wheelbase frames. They needed racing success to keep the tradition alive and encourage the "brand loyalty" that had helped them through the lean years of the Depression. It certainly did not come in the TT, with team newcomer Tim Hunt the best placed in a Senior race fourth spot. Bill Mansell was working with Joe Craig (an ex-works team rider, now involved on the racing development side) to keep the CS1 competitive as they waited for the new racing engine. 1929 ended on a low note, but feverish activity at Bracebridge Street was to pay off soon.

From Side Valve to Overhead Cam

The 1930s saw the roadster range brought up to date with changes in both styling and basic engineering. A shorter wheelbase frame brought the machines into line with the fashion that had left the long, low style of the 1920s looking dated, and the magneto was moved from the front of the engine to a platform behind the cylinder barrel; the alternative was a Lucas Magdyno for those who wanted lights. The ohv engines had their pushrods enclosed in plated tubes, sealed top and bottom with simple rubber rings, and at the same time the tappets between the cam followers and the pushrods were eliminated.

The factory was reorganised on the buying side, with parts either made "in house" or bought from an associate company if at all possible; with the Shelley works on the other side of Aston Brook Street there was the facility of both a foundry and a large machine shop and the castings came from there. Abingdon's made the new gear oil pump, while tanks and sheet metal pressings came from Tallboy's of Witton, Birmingham, and Alfred Roberts made all the rubber parts. A Norton front fork that owed a lot in its design to the Webbs used before was made in the frame shop.

Gearboxes were still bought from Sturmey Archer of Nottingham, until they stopped making motor cycle parts in 1934; Norton then bought the design rights and had them made by Burman in Birmingham. They also introduced their own clutch design, the three-spring unit that earned a reputation for longevity and the guts to withstand the heaviest of untrained feet. Or hands, because most models could be ordered with hand gear change if the customer preferred.

Arthur Carroll's ohc engine became available to the public in 1932, and Jim Simpson took over a road test model from *Motor Cycling's* man at a road outside Birmingham, then rode it through the quarter-mile at 100mph and 98.9mph on runs in either direction.

At the more mundane end of the range, the 16H and Big 4 continued through the decade. They were updated in line with the current range year by year, but never were regarded as anything but tourers, even if a euphoric test of the 71mph solo 16H by *Motor Cycling* in 1939 did headline it as a "fine example of a reliable and fast touring machine." It weighed 363lb dry, which was a lot of weight added since its day as a slim single-gear belt driver weighing just 280lb, but times had changed for simple side valves.

Apart from the development of their road machines, Norton had made been busy in the racing field, taking the European Grands Prix by storm in 1931 and remaining a force to reckon with until the end of the decade, when BMW and Gilera began to take over in the 500cc class. Occasionally the supercharged two-stroke DKWs would trespass into the 350 class and prove an embarrassment, but they generally stayed with the 250 class and were not regarded as a regular threat.

But the 1930s was an outstanding period for Norton, their winning making the name known all over the world. It is worthy of its own chapter in this story.

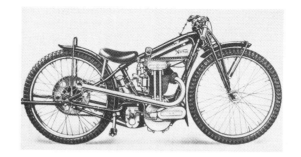

1930 SPEEDWAY MODEL. During 1930 a Speedway Model was produced, as that sport had enjoyed a boom and every manufacturer of note at some time tried to make a machine that would impress the considerable crowds that gathered around the cinder oval. Norton used a modified ES2 engine in a modified diamond frame, with Webb speedway forks and a simple countershaft mounted in a standard gearbox shell. It was not a success, as J A Prestwich of Tottenham launched their legendary speedway motor that same year and by August were quoting a peak output of 33bhp with a good spread of torque from an engine weighing just 57lb.

1931 MODEL 18. The 1931 Model 18 showed the revised layout of the roadsters well, with the rear-mounted Magdyno making the shorter wheelbase easier to achieve.

Also new was the gear oil pump, in the base of the new shape timing cover, but conveniently omitted from the artist's cutaway drawing. The exhaust pipe route along the left-hand side of the machine was no aid to access to the primary transmission and did not last long.

DUTCH SURVIVOR. One Speedway model Norton lasted in regular use into the 1980s as the mount for a Dutch "Wall of Death" performer, who seems to have kept it in remarkably original condition apart from removing the lower chainstays and the rear stand (though these were probably lost when the machine was actually being raced, as slight whipping of the frame was found to aid the sliding technique). It also seems that gears have been fitted into the box, the lever being typical of the foot (or knee) change style of the competition riders using the old Sturmey Archer gearbox.

TO THE FAR CORNERS...Nortons for export were loaded onto contractors' lorries from the Aston Brook Street loading deck, where the official title adopted after a 1926 restructuring of the finances was evidenced in the facade. Export machines were packed in wooden crates made by Arthur Gossage Ltd, with their handlebars detached and the cables still in place, felt and corrugated cardboard being used to protect enamelled parts from transit damage. During the 1930s, the company's export agents were Messrs Baker, Fay and Baker.

1933 MODEL 19. The Model 19 engine dimensions were altered for the 1933 season, from 79 x 120mm (the same bore as the 500, of course) to 82 x 113mm (the same bore as the Big 4 side valve model). The capacity increased slightly, from 588 to 596cc, but the benefit was in reduced piston speed; the 596cc overhead camshaft engine that came later was to prove very popular as a racing engine in the sidecar class.

1933 350s. A pair of 350s were added to the range for 1933, with 71 x 88mm engines offering a single exhaust port on the Model 50 and twin ports on the 55. The cycle parts were identical to the 500cc models, which gave the smaller machines a considerable weight penalty to overcome. Although they were not high performance models, they stayed in production until 1939.

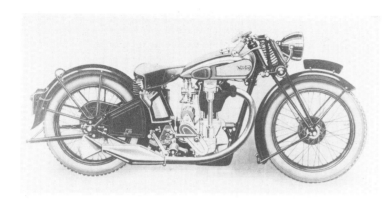

1935 MODEL 55. The 1935 Model 55 continued the twin exhaust port 350 option and was a solid, unexciting tourer with a top speed of barely 70mph. But it had its appeal as a gentle machine with everything that the man looking for reliable transport could expect. Its bigger brother was the Model 20, the twin port version of the legendary Model 18.

1936 MODEL 50. A 1936 Model 50 to trials specification. For an extra £5 the model of your choice would be fitted with the high ground clearance frame – 5 inches instead of the standard 4½ inches – unswept exhaust, wide ratio gears, 21 inch front wheel and knobbly tyres. Final assembly of all trials models was the responsibility of the foreman in charge of the assembly gang. List price for this model in the trim shown was £58 – unaltered from 1935.

1934 CS1 and MANX. The CS1 was regarded as a fast tourer, while the more recent title "International" was applied to a sports model that was readily adapted to racing. In 1934 check springs were introduced, to supplement the central barrel spring and helped to reduce frenzied pattering over small road bumps.

Although the term International was used in the company's catalogues through the 1930s, the works referred to racing specification specials as a "Manx". It arose from the job cards used on the assembly shop floor, where "Inter" meant a roadgoing sportster and "Manx" meant racing specification.

VIC BRITTAIN. Vic Brittain was Norton's leading trials competitor on solos during the 1930s and his name is remembered today in the national trial that bears his name. *Motor Cycling* analysed the machines of the top trials men in February 1939 and Vic's Norton 500 appeared to be very much like a standard machine, weighing 322lb and being based on the ES2, with a ground clearance of 5 inches. Compression ratio was 6.5:1 and gear ratios 18, 14, 9.5 and 6.2:1. Tyres were 21 inches x 2.75 at the front and 19 x 4.00 at the rear.

JACK WILLIAMS. Jack Williams of Cheltenham was also a leading rider for Norton in sporting trials, normally mounted on a 350cc Model 50. Surprisingly, his 350 weighed slightly more than Vic Brittain's 500 machine, at 325lb (147kg) to the 500's 322lb. With the whole range available to trials specification, it was good publicity for the factory to have variety of models performing under their banner, rather than concentrate on one model and suggest that it alone was the superior machine for the clubman who was a potential customer.

DENNIS MANSELL. Dennis Mansell was Norton's leading sidecar trials competitor of the era, one of many senior managers with the company who was also an active competitor. His ohc Model 30 weighed 362lb and the sidecar 142lb and was lower geared than most of his rivals with ratios of 7.25, 12.1, 17.5 and 21:1.

Dennis, here tackling Hollinsclough in the Bemrose Trial, crowned his career with a win in the 1939 British Experts trial. When regulations allowed, he used a special outfit with sidecar wheel drive and this experience was to prove very useful when the factory developed a sidecar wheel drive outfit for the military during the 1939-45 War.

COURTESY OF CASTROL. Norton did not buy an advertisement in the 1937 TT practice edition of *The Motor Cycle*, but enjoyed a full page reminder of their racing prowess with this illustration by Castrol, showing Jimmy Guthrie's 1936 500cc machine.

In the same week, applications were invited from holders of university degrees to apply for the James L Norton Scholarship, worth £140 for one year. The successful candidate would be required "to devote his whole time to the study of automobile engineering problems connected with motor cycles, and to produce a thesis at the end of the year embodying the results of his investigations."

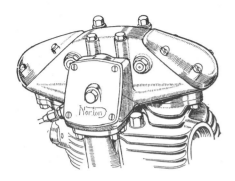

1938 BIG 4. A 1938 Big 4, on test with a Model G sidecar attached, poses with Warwick Castle as a background. The twin outlet silencer, known in the works as the "cow's udder" was fitted for the 1938 season only and did nothing for the appearance of the range, though it was efficient in terms of silence and power. The Service Department regularly replaced them in later years, when overhauling customers' machines, as they were prone to cracking at the mounting points.

EXPERIMENTAL ENGINE. Jack Williams, better known as a trials rider for the factory, used an experimental engine for the 1937 Junior TT with enclosed valve gear, the rockers accessible through caps retained by four screws. *The Motor Cycle* reported that "The new valve gear certainly retains the oil, the engine showing no signs of leakage whatsoever." Such continence would have pleased many owners of the International model, but they were never to see the style go into production.

1939 ES2. For 1939, plunger rear springing was available as an option on the ES2 at an extra £7.10.0d and another £1.10.0d would buy an International tank to add to the good looks of the machine. Henry Laird tested a rear-sprung version for *Motor Cycling* in January of that year and told how a stretch of road near Kenilworth in Warwickshire that was "interesting" on a rigid-framed machine at 65mph could be ridden at 70mph on the spring frame ES2 with ease. Even a 50-mile run with a pillion passenger was included in the report, and the passenger confirmed the improved comfort. The 396lb machine gave a top speed of 82mph on a top gear of 4.64:1 and consumed petrol at the rate of 64mpg in town and 72mpg in the country.

The Racing Legend 1931–1939

The 1930 season started badly, with the TT dominated by the 4-valve Rudges that took the first three places in the Senior and the first two in the Junior. Jimmy Simpson salvaged a little pride with third place in the Senior. The Walter Moore engine was simply not able to keep up with the opposition at that stage.

However, Arthur Carroll's new overhead camshaft engine, which owed much to the successful Velocette design, was race-ready for the 1931 season and the factory team of that year – Stanley Woods, Tim Hunt, Jimmy Guthrie and Jimmy Simpson – were to win the 350 and 500 class of every European Grand Prix as well as the TT races as Norton set about a domination of international road racing that was unequalled until the Japanese shared such success between a number of factories in the 1960s.

The architect of Norton's success was Joe Craig, who had left the company's employment and returned to the family garage business in Northern Ireland before being invited back in 1929. Working with Arthur Carroll, he saw success late in the 1930 season when Stanley Woods won the 500 class of the French and Ulster Grands Prix and Jimmy Simpson repeated the treatment in Sweden. Craig was not a designer, but a man whose talent was the recruitment and control of the best riders of the day and the refining of a sound engine design to racewinning form by the application of what he called "functional harmonization".

Dennis Mansell worked under Craig at the TT, looking after the vital pit arrangements. He has told of preparations for the 1931 races, when all the leading opposition riders were secretly timed over a 2½ mile stretch from Kates Cottage to Cronk-ny-Mona during practice. The Nortons were some 12 seconds faster over that stretch and the night before the race the team's engines had their compression ratios reduced to give an extra safety margin. Tim Hunt made history by winning both Junior and Senior races, with Nortons second and third in the Senior and second in the Junior. It was this thorough approach that helped them to succeed – a far cry from the debacle of the 1927 race, when lack of planning had contributed to Stanley Woods' retirement when leading the Senior by a handsome margin.

The team could be accurately described as "Unapproachable" in the early 1930s, although Woods became a thorn in their flesh when he decided to go freelance in 1934 – and first tested his works 500 Husqvarna by riding it in a local ice race! But Scotsman Jimmy Guthrie took over as team leader and won five TT races before crashing fatally on the last lap of the 1937 German GP; the factory withdrew their entries from the Ulster race as a mark of respect.

Foreign opposition was growing by 1935, with BMW entering supercharged flat twins and the supercharged four-cylinder Italian Rondine winning the Tripoli Grand Prix – not an event the British teams contested. Stanley Woods was riding a V-twin Moto Guzzi that year and he broke the Senior lap record to beat Jimmy Guthrie in the TT. But Nortons continued with the faithful singles, adding plunger rear suspension in 1936, then telescopic forks and double overhead camshafts in 1938. They were still winning their coveted TT trophies, with Freddie Frith taking the Senior in 1937 and Harold Daniell setting a lap record of 91.38mph that was to stand for twelve years, on his way to winning the 1938 race. But in 1939 the works team was disbanded and BMW's George Meier took the Senior TT win, the first foreign rider to do so. The Rondine was now known as the Gilera and Dorino Serafini had won the 1938 Ulster Grand Prix on it.

THE NORTON HABIT. Tim Hunt started what became known as "the Norton habit" in 1931, when he won both Senior and Junior TT races. Stanley Woods repeated the record in both 1932 and 1933, and looks remarkably fresh as he runs to congratulate Hunt on finishing second in the 1933 Junior race. Behind Tim, Arthur Carroll looks suitably pleased at another walkover for his design while Joe Craig grins quietly at another campaign completed with a 1-2-3 victory in both races. Joe's armband simply says "Competitor Attendant No. 30", an unpretentious title for the mastermind of the Norton racing operation.

1931 AUSTRALIAN SIDECAR TT. Overseas successes were not limited to the European continent, even as early as 1931. That year the Australian Sidecar TT was won by Jack Wassall on his 588cc model and he is here looking very happy with the result, while passenger Errol DeCean seems less sure about it all.

STANLEY WOODS AND TIM HUNT. The combination of Stanley Woods and Tim Hunt swept the board in the Grands Prix of 1931 and '32, winning 13 350 or 500 races between them. In the Swedish race in 1933 Hunt collided with a slower rider while shadowing Woods and suffered a badly broken leg that ended his racing career. Here Stanley leads Tim in the 1933 Dutch 500, en route to another 1-2 for Norton.

1932 SENIOR TT. Stanley Woods', Junior and Senior "double" in the 1932 TT was the first of two achieved as a member of the Norton team, every one at record speed. After the 1932 Senior, won at 79.38mph, he was congratulated by the Prince of Wales, later George VI. The bespectacled figure behind the Prince is Gilbert Smith, who joined the company in 1916 and was a major strength in their later growth. To the right, unusually in a bowler hat, designer Arthur Carroll looks suitably pleased.

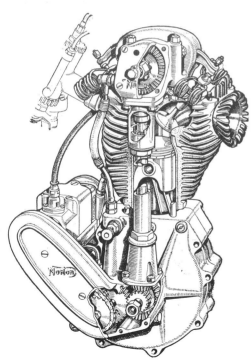

1934 TT ENGINE. For the 1934 TT, the works machines were fitted with hairpin valve springs, which enjoyed improved cooling with their coils getting a better flow of air. New also that year was the aluminium cylinder barrel with a steel liner and a cylinder head with a bronze shell around which the aluminium was cast. Jimmy Guthrie proved its worth with wins in both Junior and Senior, with Jimmy Simpson second in both races, also on a Norton.

In the same edition of *Motor Cycling* in which his drawing appeared was a report of the Grand Prix of Europe, which that year was the Dutch event. The headlines reflected the shock of the results: "No Britons finish in 500 class", in which Guthrie's Norton retired. However, Jimmy Simpson salvaged a little national pride by winning the 350 race.

MAURICE CANN. Maurice Cann, from Leicester, was a Rolls-Royce engineer and his machines were prepared to the standard that qualification suggests. He scored a Junior/Senior "double" in the 1937 Manx Grand Prix, lifting the 500 race speed over 80mph.

He rose to fame with his 1933 500cc International, seen here at Donington Park with short circuit tank and a straight-through exhaust pipe that shows evidence of some hard riding. A plug spanner in the boot was customary wear, even on short circuits.

JIMMY SIMPSON. Jimmy Simpson is best remembered as the first man to lap the TT course at 60, 70 and 80mph, but his sole victory was the 1934 250cc race on a Rudge. His ability to ride faster than most machines could last earned him something of a reputation as a machine breaker, but as a member of the Norton team from 1930 to 1934 he won the factory no less than 14 Grands Prix. His final racing year brought him more wins than any other rider, with a 350/500 "double" at the Swiss meeting and 350 wins in Belgium, Holland, Germany and Ulster, at the last of which he is seen here on his way to his last racing win. He retired from racing at the end of the 1934 season and became almost as well known as a technical representative for Castrol oil as he was as a rider.

1936 TT. The popularity of the TT Races with motor cyclists was the major reason for Nortons devoting so much effort to success there. Long before the days of portable radios receiving local broadcasts, the crowds would line the course to watch their favourites, even though the race positions were known only to the most knowledgeable, with a stopwatch. The 33rd Milestone in the 1936 TT provides evidence of this.

1936 NORTON TEAM. The Norton team for 1936 relax over copies of *The TT Special* and check the practice leaderboard. Freddie Frith is on the left, John "Crasher" White in the centre and the shy Jimmy Guthrie, team leader, on the right. Frith has warm memories of Guthrie: "Jimmy was tremendous and I learnt a lot from him."

GUTHRIE WINS 1936 SENIOR TT. Jimmy Guthrie began his TT career with second place on a New Hudson behind Alec Bennett's Norton in the 1927 Senior race. The canny Joe Craig brought him into the Norton fold in 1931, when he finished runner-up to Tim Hunt in both 350 and 500 TT races. When Stanley Woods left the team at the end of 1933 and Tim Hunt's career had been brought to a premature end by injury, Jimmy stepped into the role of team leader and went on to win a TT "double" in 1934, followed by the 1935 Junior, the 1936 Senior and the 1937 Junior. Here he takes Ballaugh Bridge during the winning 1936 Senior TT ride.

FRITH, WHITE, GUTHRIE. The Norton team went on from the Isle of Man to the round of Continental races, travelling by train with Joe Craig and two mechanics as the sole team support. In Germany they were almost overwhelmed by the 250,000 crowd, mobile workshops for the BMW and DKW teams and the Minister of Sport there to carry the flag for Hitler's Nazi government. Small was beautiful even then; Frith won the 350 race and Guthrie the 500.

SCRUTINEERING. Jimmy Guthrie presents the plunger-sprung works 500 for scrutineering before the 1936 TT, which he won at a record speed of 85.8mph. Jimmy spent his winters working at his garage in his native Hawick and in early spring a machine would be sent up to him to start his training, which he did with an early morning session on the local roads – until a friendly warning that the express trains he was in the habit of racing included passengers who were taking quite an interest in unofficial activities!

SUSPENSION AT WORK. The breathtaking dive down the bumps of Bray Hill still tests the steering of any machine, and the introduction of the plunger-sprung rear end on the works machines for the 1936 TT made life a little easier on the riders and enabled them to ride the bumpier sections faster. Guthrie, plug spanner in boot in case a quick swap is needed, demonstrates the advantage of the sprung frame as he heads for his fourth TT win in the 1936 Senior.

J.H. White "Norton" 3rd in Junior T.T. 1936

FREDDIE FRITH. A stonemason from Grimsby, Freddie Frith was signed up for the works team in 1936 and one of his first tasks was to assess the brand new spring frame. He recently recalled the impression it made: "Having ridden rigid machines in the Manx GP right up to 1935, my reaction to the rear sprung works machine in 1936 was that it was so much easier physically on the rider, a tremendous advantage on the seven lap TT, which had a few more bumps than it has today."

"CRASHER" WHITE. The original caption to this picture of John "Crasher" White dates it from 1936, but in fact it is from 1935, when the Norton team used rigid frames. White was a school-teacher from Radlett, Herts. and acquired his nickname after crashing while leading the 1933 350 Manx Grand Prix and then falling twice in the 500. In 1934 he stayed aboard to win the Junior Manx, which was an almost automatic route to a place in the Norton team.

1936 350 DUTCH TT. White rose above his "Crasher" title as a team member. He had to, because too many falls from the precious products of Joe Craig's department would see a rider looking for another employer. Here he heads towards victory in the 1936 350 Dutch TT, on the Circuit van Drenthe. In four seasons with the team, he won six Grands Prix and was a consistent leaderboard finisher.

FRITH'S FIRST TT. Frith's first TT race was a controversial one, though not for him. When team leader Guthrie had a chain come off while leading the race, Freddie took over and won, with race and lap records. Guthrie was excluded for allegedly receiving outside assistance, but after a protest was reinstated to the fifth place he finished in after being black flagged and was paid the prize money for second place. Norton won the Manufacturer's Team Prize after the protest was settled, as J H White had finished second to Frith.

Here Freddie is congratulated by Bill Mansell, then Chairman of Norton Motors. Joe Craig is hidden behind Freddie, third finisher Ted Mellors (Velocette) is to the right in leathers and behind him is Norton race mechanic Bill Mewis – who spent his weekends as passenger to Dennis Mansell.

1936 350. "Crasher" White on his 1936 350 for the TT. The roadgoing ohc models had a different bottom cradle that year, with the front curved upwards to slightly increase ground clearance, but the works machine retained the old lower cradle. The fork check springs visible (and on the team picture on page 39) are straight, whereas the roadster versions were barrel shaped. The front number plate mounts on the mudguard hint at how the running-in was done.

CHARACTERISTIC STYLE. Freddie Frith's characteristic style was to lean the bike in and keep his body upright. Here he takes Quarter Bridge in the 1936 Junior TT, in the days before the café was built on the corner. The girder forks and plunger rear springing of that year and the next gave "excellent handling, in some respects superior to the telescopics introduced in 1938", he recalls.

JOHNNY LOCKETT. Johnny Lockett was a leading Manx Grand Prix competitor from 1936, when he was fifth in the Junior race and went on to finish third in the 1937 Junior and runner-up in the 1938 Senior, the last of the series before the Second World War.

In the 1938 races, Johnny used Francis Beart's engine in his own frame. During the 1950s he was rewarded with a works team place, but he never managed to win an Island race.

HAROLD DANIELL. Harold Daniell was an unlikely looking hero, but his determined riding of the works Nortons became a legend in the factory's history. In the 1938 Senior TT, he came up from third place on the fourth lap to tie with Freddie Frith for second place at the end of the fifth. But the leader was Stanley Woods on a Velocette and Harold wasn't having that! He took the lead on the sixth lap with a new record and on his final lap went around in 24 minutes 52.6 seconds (an average of 91.0mph) to set a record that was unbroken until 1950. When Harold volunteered as a despatch rider during the coming war, he failed his eyesight test!

PRE-RACE INSTRUCTIONS. Frith receives instructions from Joe Craig before the start of the 1938 Senior TT, in which he finished third to Harold Daniell (Norton) and only 1.6 second behind Stanley Woods (Velocette).

1939 was the first year of telescopic forks on Nortons; they gave 2½ inches of movement and a better action under heavy braking. Frith's suggestion of the reason behind their move to teles is worth recording, since he was one of the riders charged with testing them originally: "At that time telescopics were becoming fashionable and I suspected that cosmetic changes influenced Norton's decision to change."

1938 was also the first year that a double overhead camshaft Norton engine raced in the TT. Although the press acclaimed the 1937 works machines as having twin camshafts, they were in fact single camshaft engines with long rockers occupying the space that outsiders assumed was occupied by spur gears.

45

1938 SWISS GRAND PRIX. On the left Joe Craig wears a satisfied smile. Not surprising, because Harold Daniell has just won the 1938 500cc Swiss Grand Prix at Geneva, having won the 350 race earlier. Freddie Frith was runner-up in both events.

The Swiss was the only 500cc European Grand Prix won by a Norton that year, the supercharged BMWs of Georg Meier and Jock West proving too fast for the singles. In fact, Meier won four of the five 500cc GPs – a sign of growing domination by the multis.

1938 JUNIOR TT. Harold Daniell was the hero of the 1938 TT races with his outstanding 91.00mph lap in winning the Senior race. He had less luck in the Junior race, where the fast Velocettes of Stanley Woods and Ted Mellors took first and second, with the slim and light Freddie Frith third on the best Norton finisher.

Harold came into his own when wrestling the bigger machine, which was not so affected by his weight as the 350. His press-on style still comes over as he pushes his Junior mount through Union Mills, but even his determination was not enough to overcome the speed penalty.

KEN BILLS. The Manx Grand Prix series ended its pre-war run in 1938, with Ken Bills winning both Junior and Senior races at record speeds and with record laps in both races. Ken was an optician, from Gillingham, Kent, and when the Manx started again in 1946 he won the Junior race and was second in the Senior. This picture of Ken on his way to winning the 1938 Junior race shows how the TT course was still a country road in parts; this is the approach to The Nook, on the outskirts of Douglas. The elastic bands around the rider's arms and thighs were an attempt to keep the bulky racing leathers of the period from flapping in the breeze and affecting top speed.

REG DEARDEN. Reg Dearden of Manchester was renowned for his generosity in entering young up-and-comers and established riders in both the TT and the Manx Grand Prix on a host of Nortons. His enthusiasm for the Isle of Man races was born of his own experience there, though he never managed to feature in the first three in the results. As he swoops through Kate's Cottage during the 1937 Senior Manx Grand Prix, he has the road to himself and the attention of all onlookers.

When Nortons were finally moved out of Bracebridge Street, Reg was said to have bought the contents of the racing department for £1000.

596cc COMBINATION. Ferdinand Aubert on a 596cc combination was Switzerland's leading sidecar racer in the 1930s. Here on his way to winning the 1937 International Grand Prix of Geneva, he was also runner-up in the Grand Prix d'Europe in Berne that year, beaten only by the works DKW of Braun. Aubert's sidecar was unusual in having the passenger lean out on left-handers in a prone position ahead of the sidecar wheel; the accepted style of the period was for passengers to straddle the sidecar mudguard when steering to port.

DONINGTON 1939. At the *Motor Cycling* meeting at Donington Park in May, 1939, Johnny Lockett was second in the 500cc race on Francis Beart's machine. Its usual immaculate turnout was a centre of attention in the paddock and its slim short-circuit tank and airscoop on the front brake typified the thoroughness of Beart's preparation.

LATVIAN CHAMPION. Arthur Pops of Latvia raced this Model 30 International in the late 1930s and became the Latvian champion in 1946 and 47 on the same machine. Just how he got hold of a plunger sprung frame is not known, but enthusiasts in the Russian bloc are renowned for their ingenuity in using what is to hand to keep their machines running, so it may be a roadster frame. Arthur is here about to take part in an old machine parade – proof of the attraction of old motor cycles and the long life of Nortons.

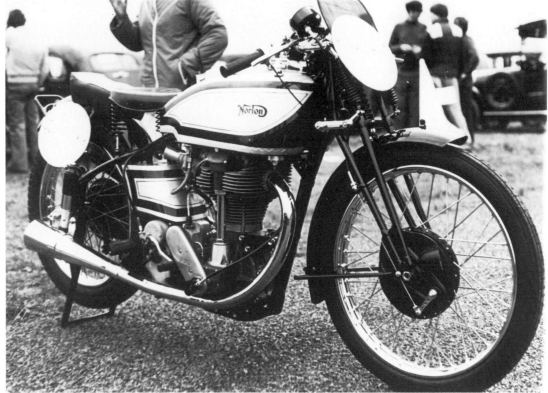

BEART'S NORTONS. Donington Park, May 1939 and Francis Beart loads his Nortons on the trailer after another successful day. The towing vehicle is that rare and desirable car, a Vauxhall 30/98. The 500cc machine, number 51, shows evidence of much lightening work on the rear suspension.

1939 PRIVATEER. The factory had no official entries for the 1939 TT races, concentrating their efforts on production of the 16H for the military. But a special batch of six Internationals to Manx specification were supplied to leading private owners and this beautiful 350 was ridden by

Harley Deschamps, who retired after falling at the Quarry Bends on the second lap. It has been restored by Manx resident John Flood, who has Deschamps' original crash helmet and gloves with the machine.

1939 SIDECAR OUTFIT. At the August Bank Holiday meeting at Donington Park in 1939, Len Taylor created a great deal of interest by riding a sidecar outfit with rear suspension, one of the very early instances of a racing sidecar having anything other than a rigid frame. It was effective, Taylor finishing second in his class, beaten only by circuit specialist Arthur Horton, on another 596cc overhead camshaft Norton.

The factory withdrew official support of racing at the end of the 1938 season. Gilbert Smith wrote later: "Our racing machines had to be made in the tool-room, but at the same time we were being pressed by H M Government to duplicate jigs and tools for the manufacture of machines for the War Office. We simply could not duplicate all these jigs and tools in the time allotted to us and at the same time produce machines for the TT." So the humble 16H took priority over the glamorous racing machinery and the factory busied itself for the threatened war.

The works machines were loaned to Harold Daniell and Freddie Frith, but they could not bring a TT win home to the hard-working factory. Harold was second to Stanley Woods (Velocette) by just eight seconds in the Junior race and Freddie was a gallant third in the Senior, unable to live with the sheer speed of the blown BMWs of Meier and West. In the

500cc Ulster Grand Prix of 1938 he had been leading when Serafini on the supercharged Gilera came by, grinned at him, then took a handful of throttle and disappeared; Freddie estimated the speed difference between the two machines at something near 20mph!

Joe Craig left the company and went to BSA, who were thinking of entering international racing when peace returned. "BSAs will be there" forecast the headline over an article bearing Joe's name that appeared in *Motor Cycling* during December 1939, but it was not to be. Joe went from BSA to the AMC factory in London, where he was one of the team working on the parallel twin that was to be their contender when racing started again. The AJS "Porcupine" was to be a threat to the Norton supremacy in the 1940s, when Craig was once more back on the Bracebridge Street payroll. But that was in the future; first of all there was a war to be won.

Bracebridge Street Goes to War

In December 1935, few could have forecast the terrible war that was to come in 1939. But it was that early when the Norton factory made its first notable inroad into the military market.

Comparative tests were made by the Mechanical Warfare Experimental Establishment to select a suitable machine to replace the V-twin BSA that was standard issue at that time. Their report B18/30 of 17th December 1935, marked "Secret", lists eight machines that were tested against the BSA, over road and cross-country courses with between 2200 and 4500 miles covered initially. The first paragraph of the report put the final nail firmly in the old BSA's coffin when it said of all the machines "...all were more pleasant to ride than the control BSA". It went on to dent some fine reputations, thus: "The two Royal Enfields and the BSA have given a good deal of trouble on account of engine failures."

"Of the 500cc machines, the best is the Norton..." they concluded, though the 350 Matchless was considered its equal. The 16H is recorded as weighing 378lb and giving 56.8mpg while averaging 34.2mph over a 100-mile road circuit. By December 1936 a report of a test on a 500cc Rudge was "...in competition with the WD-pattern Norton single cylinder motor cycle." So the 16H was the military's standard machine three years before Europe was thrown by Adolf Hitler's ambition into one of its darkest periods. Not

that everyone had recognised that conflict was coming; in April of that year "Carbon" of *Motor Cycling* thought it was all a bit of a scare: "My opinion, for what it is worth, is that there won't be a war. I do not even believe that there is much likelihood of a crisis that would upset trade for the time being..." But Gilbert Smith, Managing Director of Norton, was more farsighted and the factory swung over to production of the 16H, then followed that up with the Big 4 sidecar with two-wheel drive.

The job of liaison with the military authorities during the tests of the 16H had been the responsibility of Howard Drake, and his name appears in reports as modifications were tested at later stages. But with the declaration of war Alan Wilson was promoted from his previous post as chief tester to oversee the military liaison and two Inspectors from the A.I.D. were based at the factory, with the authority to visit any department and check the work. On one occasion they ticked off engine timer "Pop" Swinnerton because a machine back from random road test had blued its exhaust. From then on, if a road test sample wanted its ignition timed, Pop would send a junior down to do it.

Not all machines were road tested, as fuel was in very short supply. Instead, engines were run-in for 20 minutes on a bench, fuelled by a pipe from the town gas supply. The road testers were kept on, to check machines picked

at random; they were also members of the factory's Home Guard, unit and would sometimes ride home on a test 16H, have a quick meal before doing a night's duty as a local despatch rider, then take breakfast before reporting back for a day's work.

The Service Department was kept busy dealing with major rebuilds that could not be handled by the military workshops; they mended frames, but forks were sent by the works Big 4 sidecar hack to the W H Drew works in Conybere Street. The 16H model was no problem to sort out, but the sidecar-wheel-drive Big 4 is recalled by at least one of the fitters as "a major nightmare".

It was during the war that the production was changed from the rather piecemeal method of separate crews on their own benches to a line system. Benches that stretched the length of the ground floor assembly shop were installed and machines built up progressively as they went from one end of the benches to the other. Joe Bates was recruited from the BSA factory to set up and supervise this system, and his efforts contributed to a remarkable level of output. Estimates suggest that the Bracebridge Street works turned out 100,000 machines between 1939 and 1945 – an average of 320 machines a week.

ARMY REGISTER. The Press rose to the occasion and worked hard to get active motor cyclists to make themselves available for enlistment, normally offering their own machines as a contribution to the war effort. Thousands filled in such a form as this and soon found themselves "on the strength".

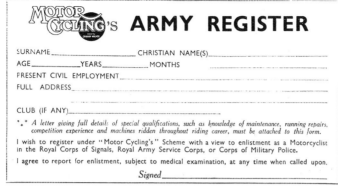

21,000 MOTOR CYCLES. There were some 21,000 motor cycles on the Army's strength when war was declared, including over 6000 civilian machines either impressed for military use or owned by the volunteers who had signed up in response to a patriotic campaign run in the motor cycle press. One unit had machines ranging from a 500cc Triumph twin to a modest 98cc autocycle.

By June 1949 there were 50,000 machines in service, with Norton the leading supplier and dominating this official picture. Captions were all approved by the Official Censor before release and gave little information, this one simply saying: "Large numbers of Army motorcyclists on powerful motor cycles and all armed with Tommyguns are now an important part of Britain's Army. This picture taken in Eastern Command, shows them taking part in an exercise."

PERILOUS PURSUIT. An ES2 with its original 1938 "cow's udder" silencer is used to demonstrate an ingenious solo mounting for a tommy gun, as a member of the 1st Battalion Grenadier Guards keeps watch near Swanage, Dorset, in 1941.

A strut from the saddle nose had a lockable swivel mount for the gun. It may have been a practical idea on tarmac roads, but firing accurately whilst riding across country must have taxed the rider's skills somewhat.

BRISTLING WITH GUNS. The Norton reputation for strength was put to the test in training of raw recruits in the black art of sidecar driving, in combat and even when posing for official pictures. With steam rising from the exhaust pipe and the driver slipping the clutch, a Big 4 outfit claws through a watersplash. The grab handle on the extended front mudguard stay provides evidence of the conditions the outfit would be rescued from on occasions and the crew look suitably fearless for the benefit of the camera.

BIG 4 COMBINATION. The 633cc Big 4 outfit drove the sidecar wheel via a shaft from a simple dog clutch on the special rear spindle. Drive was engaged or disengaged by a lever behind the driver's left leg and the dog clutch was protected by a press-studded leather gaiter that had to be removed every week and packed with grease.

The tool kit for the Big 4 was extensive and included a jack, to make the wheel changing quicker.

The spare wheel – both front and rear mountings for it were used – was interchangeable with all three others. Lighting was modest, with the 24 watt main bulb shrouded by the hood that prevented the spread of light upwards, where it might be spotted by enemy aircraft. In convoy, drivers kept station in the dark by keeping the white-painted tail of the rear mudguard (or axle, in the case of a lorry) in view.

NORTONS IN BEIRUT.
Australian Don Rs head a convoy into Beirut as Allied troops arrive during the summer of 1941, their exposed rear chains having survived the rigours of the Middle East climate and sand. The 16H was used by troops from Canada, too, and in 1943 their despatch riders in Sicily were covering an average of 2000 miles a week. One UK-based unit used carrier pigeons as a supplement to normal communications, carrying the birds six at a time in a special back pack.

SUNK! The Big 4 with two wheels driven could cope with most terrains – but there were limits. This Canadian driver was described in the caption as "roaring through a swamp…right into a deep water bog", which suggests warmer climes that would not encourage the crew to wear gloves and greatcoats.

The picture gives a clear view of the Bren gun mounting on the sidecar, with spring damping front and rear. The sidecar seat offers very little comfort, but later versions came with padding to seat and backrest. For the pillion passenger there was a second saddle with a substantial grab handle to give security on rough terrain.

The outfit was replaced by the 4-wheel-drive Jeep, which had greater carrying capacity and proved far easier for novice drivers to handle. The need to disengage sidecar wheel drive on the road was not always remembered by newly trained men and this was behind the decision to cut off the sidecar wheel drive when the outfits were sold off in peacetime.

MEMORIES OF PEACETIME. The factory was busy with the production of basic transport, and with petrol strictly rationed to those with essential jobs to do, there was very little private motoring. Yet Norton did buy advertising in the weekly journals, as other makers did.

This 1942 front cover of *Motor Cycling* was still making use of the racing successes of 1938 to remind motor cyclists that Norton meant more than the staid mounts they were compelled to ride – if they were lucky enough to even ride.

Apart from nostalgic articles of sporting events of the past, the editorial in this edition reported the Pretoria Grand Prix in South Africa, where Nortons won every race apart from the 250. It was not quite like the TT course familiar to most readers; V Bosch was reported as having to retire when his crankcase was smashed by a stone.

TOUGH CONDITIONS. Those in the desert campaigns wished for rain, while those in northern Europe must have longed for a little sun and sand. The advantage of a solo motor cycle in extreme conditions was that muscle power stood a chance of rescuing it from most situations, as a friendly Dutch native shows during a rainy season in 1944.

The standard service routine for the 16H reflected the thoroughness of the military approach to keeping vehicles running in all conditions. Weekly maintenance covered removing Bowden cables, checking free movement and lubricating; lubricating control levers, and greasing nipples on front forks (6 in all), rebound springs (4), head races (2), and one each on speedometer drive, front brake cam spindle, rear brake lever pivot and gear change lever.

Every 3000 miles chains had to be correctly tensioned, the primary chaincase removed and cleaned out while the lift (sic) on the mainshaft was checked. After the magneto chain was also checked there were all nuts and bolts to be checked for tightness.

By the end of hostilities the total Army strength of motor cycles had reached 270,000 – almost 40% of them Nortons.

A MILITARY TRIBUTE. In the latter part of the War, Norton along with other makers were beginning to subtly remind future buyers that there would be motor cycles available when the conflict was over. Civilian buyers would naturally want reliability and the performance of a machine through the rigours of war was proof of what they could expect in more leisurely times.

Norton favoured using letters from anonymous members of known regiments, such as this one from a Royal Signalman in Germany. BSA's style was to describe the writer of such letters as "Jack Service" and explain to readers that he was "the symbol of the young motorised British Army."

But throughout the war period, the only civilian machines to remind the customers about were those of the 1930s – unless there could be a hint of what was to come. A little artistic licence could be excused, and this advertisement from May 1945 shows how that was applied, with a road model featuring the same style of telescopic forks as the works racing machines had worn in 1938, readily identified by the sleeve nut above the lower yoke. The mounting on the bottom of the fork leg for the mudguard stays appears to have used any artistic licence even more, with an extension of the leg beyond the spindle mounting to accommodate the stay bolt.

In truth, these early teles were not used on any production roadsters, the famous "Roadholder" forks becoming the standard item once all the stocks of girder forks had been absorbed.

INDIAN VISITORS. The performance of their 16H models impressed the Indian regiment, and when they visited Britain in 1946 their representatives asked to see where the machines were made. They met a number of factory personnel on arrival in Bracebridge Street, and from right to left the civilians are Fred Bartley (draughtsman) hiding Edgar Franks (designer), Harry Mason (draughtsman), Howard Drake (personal assistant to Gilbert Smith), and racing engine specialist Frank Sharratt.

RARE INTERIOR. Inside the factory the Indian visitors could see the assembly tracks that were installed during the war; the 16H model Frank Sharratt is looking over being mounted on a small wheeled trolley that was pushed along the track as assembly progressed. Very few photographs of the factory interior were allowed and this is a rare glimpse of the heart of the legend, taken by employee Syd Lucas.

With the war over, the industry had to adapt from the relatively easy production of single models to the more complex choice the civilian buyers would want. Most recognised that more sophisticated designs would be the road to success, just as Triumph's twin had shown in the last years of the pre-war period. Norton was one of several factories working on such a design.

The press concentrated on forecasting trends to come and advising how to get the most out of the meagre petrol allowance a lucky few had during the early months after hostilities ceased; even those prepared to risk a little shady deal on the flourishing black market appreciated tips on how to make it last longer.

Norton's published advice was to check cycle parts for free running, ensure there were no petrol leaks and above all use gentle driving techniques. To whet buying appetites, CW wrote in *Motor Cycling* of the enjoyment he had experienced in twenty years and listed amongst his stable a 1935 500 International and another of the same model from 1939, this a rare rear-sprung model which had "proved itself possibly the best road-holder I ever straddled, superby comfortably withal".

The need for machines was there. The factory set about meeting it.

The 1940s – a Time for Change

Postwar production began with old stock used wherever possible. The 16H was naturally continued, the old jigs dusted off and the more glamorous models reintroduced as quickly as practical, although early supplies were destined for the export market.

Racing was not so difficult to restart as this position suggests. Through yet another outstanding piece of longsightedness, the Norton depot in the Isle of Man had been left there intact, and spares for riders in the 1946 Grand Prix were readily available; a few fortunates had the new telescopic fork, but they were new enough not to need spares so early in their racing lives. The works machines had been stored at Nigel Spring's home in Brigg, Lincolnshire, during the war and were brought back to Birmingham to be made ready for battle. Joe Craig was back after his brief stay with BSA and AMC, but there was some difference of opinion at top level about what was the best route to take for racing success. Craig remained certain that his beloved singles could still win, whereas Gilbert Smith was making moves towards a multi. The single was due to find success in the short term, since the supercharged BMWs and Gileras were no longer allowed in international racing. But Moto Guzzi still had their V-twin, which was no sluggard, and Gilera were redesigning their Four to comply with the new FIM regulations. And in 1947, the AJS "Porcupine" twin was announced, a model due to give Joe's runners a struggle in the races ahead.

1946 MODEL 18. Norton's agent in San Francisco, California, was Al Fergoda, who was happy to show friends on the local Muir Beach the first of the 1946 Model 18s to arrive. That and the 16H were the first road models back into production, both using the cradle frame. Normal home market models did not have the luxury of chrome-plated mudguard stays, rear stand and return spring, but the Americans were export customers and got what they wanted.

SHELSLEY WALSH 1946.
Freddie Frith on a works Norton in October 1946, at the Shelsley Walsh hill climb. The works Nortons were a star attraction, their presence arranged by Gilbert Smith, as a gesture to Raymond Mays, who was involved with the organisation of the meeting. Gilbert was talking with Mays at the time about the development of a four cylinder engine to match the foreign threat, and Mays was closely involved with ERA (English Racing Automobiles) and also in the foundation of the British Racing Motor (BRM) concern.

TWIN DESIGN. In the early years after the Second World War, the success of the Triumph parallel twin in the late 1930s was remembered by all major manufacturers, and they drew up their own variations on that theme. For Norton, designer Edgar Franks drew up a design for an in-line twin, in the style of the Sunbeam that BSA were working on at that time. But it was rejected as a concept and the design department was told to produce something more conventional.

This design was drawn up by Jack Moore, and featured separate camshafts in the manner of the Triumph twin, with through bolts passing from the cylinder head via the drilled barrel and into the crankcase. Valve gear was carried in cast alloy rocker boxes, with access for tappet adjustment through side plates retained by one knurled-head screw. The cycle parts in the factory mock-up are simply standard production items; the model was not built, as Bert Hopwood joined Norton in 1947 and his own version of a parallel twin was developed.

No further record of this project can be found; it was set aside and the single camshaft Hopwood design, much like the BSA A10 but with the camshaft across the front of the engine, was put into production of 1948. It was destined to carry on, in various capacities, for many years.

KEN BILLS. Ken Bills carried on where he left off when the Manx Grand Prix started again in 1946. On a Steve Lancefield-prepared Norton with the new "Roadholder" forks fitted he won the Junior race at 74.18mph compared with his 1938 record speed of 78.76. The difference was down to the fuel, 78 octane fuel being used in 1946 and 50/50 petrol/benzole in 1938.

In the very wet Senior race Ken was second to Ernie Lyons on the new Grand Prix Triumph twin, who had two minutes in hand at the finish. Advising Ernie was that man Stanley Woods – still a thorn in the Norton Flesh!

RAYMOND MAYS, HAROLD DANIELL. At that same Shelsley Walsh event, Harold Daniell rode the pre-war International prepared by his brother-in-law Steve Lancefield, but it was not the best tool for hill climbing and the best he could manage was fourth. The Norton entries of Johnny Lockett, Freddie Frith and Harold all finished slower than Raymond Mays' RD4 ERA, but Ernie Lyons on the new Grand Prix Triumph was not so diplomatic and beat Mays' hill record with 39.44 seconds.

The open bonnet of the ERA suggests that Harold may have been asking some questions about four cylinder engines, even if the Norton/ERA talks were still on the secret list.

OILY MANX. Only the very best-prepared Manx models could be expected to keep all the oil inside. The chain oiler could produce some interesting results when its output reached the back tyre, but despite this example of the weakness this one took P M Aitchinson to finish second to Ken Bills in the 1946 Junior Manx GP. He was tragically killed on the fourth lap of the Senior race when he fell at the 33rd Milestone in very wet conditions.

DO NOT TOUCH! Winning TT races was something to boast about and the factory would lend the precious trophies to agents for display in their showrooms. The inevitable result was an invasion by possible customers of the future who could not resist the temptation to try a real racing Norton for size, despite the large "Please Do Not Touch" notice. The works machines were not loaned for these local shows, and the Manx here is a private machine with the top fork shrouds removed.

STAR CUSTOMER. Lancashire comedian George Formby was a very popular star who enjoyed getting away from the pressures of show business on a motor cycle. In 1947 he collected his new 500cc International Model 30 from Bracebridge Street and was seen off by Gilbert Smith (in the trilby hat) and next to him sales manager Leslie Hepburn. This actual machine is still in good running order, now owned by Alan Whitehead of Bolton.

1947 SENIOR TT. For Harold Daniell the 1947 Senior TT brought his second victory in the blue riband of road racing, after a tussle with team-mate Artie Bell. Bell started the last lap just one second ahead, but Harold was in front at the flag, winning by 22 seconds. Artie congratulates Harold, who partly obscures Steve Lancefield, with a happy Gilbert Smith in his customary trilby hat and a smiling Joe Craig next to him.

The Junior race had not been a good one for Nortons, with Bob Foster leading four Velocettes home and all the works Norton men retiring. The first Bracebridge Street product to finish in that race was private entrant Les Newman's, in fifth place.

NORTON ON LOCATION.
Nortons were good enough for
the most famous of people. In
MGM's *Bhowani Junction*, filmed
in Pakistan, Bill Travers played a
railway official and relied on a
16H for transport when not on a
train. Stewart Granger and Ava
Gardner seem unimpressed to be
in such dignified company.

PRIVATE OWNER. Nortons
remained the favourite 500cc
machine with private owners
competing in Continental races,
but they frequently had to work
hard to stay ahead of the growing
Italian threat. Here, Belgian
Auguste Goffin fights off a
challenge from the Swiss Musy,
mounted on a horizontal single
cylinder Moto Guzzi, as they
corner on typical Belgian pavé.
The plunger-sprung Manx was
quite a frame breaker, and riders
racing abroad became adept at
repairing fractured saddle tubes.

1950 DOMINATOR. The Dominator was first shown to the public at the Earls Court Show in November 1948, but deliveries did not start in the home market until late in 1949, early production being reserved for the export market.

Cycle parts were readily identifiable as standard Norton, with the 7 inch front brake giving a level of stopping performance that could be politely described as "adequate", but when compared with the likes of the Vincent-HRD's twin drum brake it was definitely not impressive. Black cycle parts set off the chromed tank with silver panels outlined in black with a delicate highlighting red inner line. Wheel rims were chrome, with silver painted centre unlined.

The first Norton twin for over 30 years provided a level of performance comparable with the more obviously sporting International with less mechanical clatter and less inclination to lubricate its rider, the rocker gear being completely enclosed! Although seen as a flexible tourer when first introduced, its arrival sounded the death knell of the much loved, but very dated, Inters.

1949 500T. At the 1948 Earls Court show a new trials model was announced, the 500T. It replaced the special-order Model 18 which had carried on the pre-war tradition of offering a mildly altered road machine to the competition rider. The work of the McCandless brothers, Rex and Cromie, it used the basic 16H diamond frame of WD pattern, with special fork yokes to give better trail and a wheelbase shortened from 56 to 53 inches. Wide ratio gears were fitted and the front hub had the spoke flanges scalloped.

An early customer was Birmingham's Olga Kevelos, who rode WHA 728 to a Gold Medal in the Wales-based International Six Days Trial in 1949, losing no marks.

EXTRAS. The Dominator was not to every rider's liking in standard trim and there was no shortage of extras to help modification to individual taste. Dual seats were becoming the fashion in 1949 and this Feridax version combined with the same company's windscreen to make touring more comfortable.

1949 SENIOR TT. Harold Daniell was back in the winner's circle at the 1949 Senior TT, averaging 86.93mph on the Pool petrol that entrants were still obliged to use. The "World's Best Roadholder" legend that the factory used in its advertising at the time did not truly apply to the racing machines of the late 1940s, which required Daniell's brand of muscular power to keep on the road at racing speeds. This was a rather lucky win, the AJS twin of Les Graham suffering a magneto problem when leading the race on the last lap.

1949 SENIOR TT MOUNT. Daniell's 1949 Senior TT mount at rest, showing the experimental forks with large hollow wheel spindle carried in front of the legs. At the rear end, hydraulic damping of the plunger suspension with supplementary units was an improvement on the original development, but the engine was generally proving too fast for the cycle parts. Despite the talents of Daniell and Artie Bell, the newly-introduced World Championship went to Les Graham (AJS) in the 500cc class, while Freddie Frith on Nigel Spring's Velocette won every round of the 350cc series. Nortons were demonstratably falling behind the opposition.

GEOFF DUKE. There was a bright young star in Norton's firmament as the 1940s drew to a close. They had signed up a young trials rider by the name of Geoffrey Duke and part of the deal was that he could go racing. After showing good form in the 1948 Manx Grand Prix he won the Senior Clubman's TT of 1949 at record speed, then went on to finish second in the Junior Manx Grand Prix before winning the Senior with new race and lap records. Here Geoff dives down Bray Hill on his way to a winning average of 86.06mph in the Manx.

As the 1949 season ended, it was time to take stock. Nortons needed racing success to convince the buying public that their roadsters had a racing pedigree that was not out of date. In the first official World Championships they had failed to get a man in the first three of either 350 or 500cc series; their sole success was Eric Oliver's win in the Sidecar series. But his girder-forked, rigid framed 596cc double overhead camshaft mount could not be related to the current developments in their road machines.

There was much time spent with the ERA/BRM car racing factories, and Joe Craig had even given up the day-to-day running of the racing team to carry on development work on a four-cylinder engine, the team being looked after in his absence by Steve Lancefield. But the Norton four cylinder engine was destined never to race, because another revolution came their way in the form of an all-welded duplex cradle frame designed by the McCandless Brothers of Belfast; early tests had shown that it could restore the Norton name as an outstanding handler, and with the traditional engine further strengthened to give reliable power, it was a single cylinder machine that was to carry their hopes in the 1950s.

There was a promising new member of the racing team in Geoff Duke, and with his enthusiasm combined with the experience of proven winners like Harold Daniell and Artie Bell, plus the ever reliable Johnny Lockett in a supporting role, they had the men. All they had to do was prove that they had the machinery to match that assembly of riding talent.

The range of roadsters was selling, even if it did include such old faithfuls as the perennial Big 4 and 16H. What the public could see at the end of 1949 was not very exciting, but behind the scenes were plans to put the Norton name right back at the top of the tree.

A New Era and New Stars

The 1950s dawned as an exciting era for Britain. Rationing was being eased, prosperity was in sight and engineering lessons from the past war were being applied to civilian use – in 1952 the De Havilland Comet was the first passenger jet aircraft to fly.

Norton's own contribution to the growth of modern technology was modest but effective – the Featherbed frame. It started as a racing unit and swept the board at the TT races with Geoff Duke confirming his remarkable ability as a rider. In 1951 the first road machine using the new frame was shown at Earls Court. The Dominator de luxe was the established 500cc twin in new clothes and only for export at that time; the production Manx racing machines were the only ones the public could hope to have – if they were proven racing men.

In 1952 the No. 88 Dominator de luxe was on the home market, at £265.15.7d and the flagship of the range; the rest of the Bracebridge Street products came with either rigid or plunger sprung frames and showed their long heritage. The public wanted spring frames, at least swinging fork frames and at best Featherbed frames. But Norton did not have the facilities to make the all-welded Featherbed. They were dependant upon Reynolds Tubes to make them, and the most Reynolds could make at that time was 70 units per week. Bracebridge Street needed 110 machines sold per week to break even and the dramatically reduced sales of the other models did not make up the difference.

An overnight marathon by Bob Collier in the Experimental Department produced a swinging fork adaption of the old lugged frame and once proven it was rushed into the range for 1953. But the losses incurred in 1952 made Norton Motors vulnerable and a merger with Associated Motor Cycles of London (makers of AJS and Matchless and owners of the James and Francis Barnett names) was announced in February 1953.

Gilbert Smith, the blunt outspoken man who had joined Pa Norton as a lad in 1916 and had risen to become Managing Director, continued at the head in Bracebridge Street, but it was no secret that he had little love for his new masters. His Norton colleagues had sufficient regard for Gilbert to make a special presentation to him in December 1952 to mark his 36 years of service to the company, but the coming alliance was to bring internal friction and prove a drain on the profits that Norton did make later in the decade.

1950 JUNIOR TT. Artie Bell's first works ride was in 1947. Before practice for the TT, he would recite the sequence of corners to his wife as she read a description of the course; it was typical of his thorough approach to racing. He gave the Featherbed Norton its first TT win with the 1950 Junior race, beating Geoff Duke to set a new race record at 86.33mph. Harold Daniell was third to make it a Norton 1-2-3 for the new machine's TT debut.

Here Artie takes Braddan Bridge during his record ride. He was seriously injured in the 500cc Belgian Grand Prix later in the season and never raced again.

1950 FEATHERBED. This was the machine that kept the single cylinder Manx engine ahead of almost everything in 1950 and beyond – the Featherbed, posing for the camera in the Bracebridge Street works as a white sheet hides the truth beyond from prying eyes.

Developed by the McCandless brothers, it featured sif-bronze welded construction of its duplex cradle, the tank sitting on the widely spaced top tubes and retained by a single strap from steering head to seat nose.

The engine was improved, too. The cylinder head was aluminium, with inserted valve seats of cast iron, the finning now arranged diagonally across the top and high and vertical in the area of the exhaust port. The cambox was mounted more rigidly and incorporated the revcounter drive, a less vulnerable arrangement than the magneto drive used before.

The frames were not made at Bracebridge Street, where the established skills were in lugs and brazing. Indeed, fabrications like the rear brake pedal and thin tube gear lever were cut and bent in the Experimental Department and then taken across the road to Arthur Westwood's shop to be welded.

For 1951 the Manx Norton was available with the new frame, to selected riders of proven ability only. There was a long queue of hopefuls who wanted to be ahead of the opposition, even at a whopping £429.6.8d.

DUKE AND THE FEATHERBED. It would be difficult to overstate the effect that Geoff Duke had upon the British racing scene as a member of the Norton racing team. From his first appearance on the new Featherbed frame he was winning; starting at Blandford Camp in Dorset he set a new lap record at the model's first public appearance and after his TT success was hot favourite for the 500cc World Championship. But tyre trouble hit both the Norton and AJS teams and thrown treads forced Geoff out of the Belgian and Dutch Grands Prix while up on the leaderboard. A change to Avon rubber for the Ulster Grand Prix saw him finish first and he did the same at the Italian Grand Prix, beating Masetti's Gilera on its home ground. But Umberto Masetti took the championship by one mark. In the 350 series, Geoff was again runner-up, this time to Bob Fosters Velocette. It was a remarkable debut for the young man from St Helens and his name became a household word – which did Norton no harm at all.

OFF-ROAD DUKE. Geoff Duke mixed his road racing with other branches of the sport and remained a member of the trials team during 1950, winning the Premier Award in the Victory Trial and here in the process of winning the 500cc Gibbs Cup in the Cotswold, on a 500T. He still rode in trials in 1951, but road racing was the major interest by then and a youngster was brought into the Norton team who was to become a great name in off-road sport – Jeff Smith.

HAROLD DANIELL. 1950 was Harold Daniell's last season before he retired to concentrate on his retail business in London's Forest Hill area. It was typical of him that he had the plaster cast taken off an arm broken in an early-season scrap with Duke and had a plastic brace fitted so that he could ride. Despite the handicap he was third in the Junior, in which race he is here taking flight over Ballaugh Bridge; in the Senior he was fifth.

Harold has been credited with coining the name Featherbed for the new frame, saying after a test ride: "It's like riding a b..... featherbed." A master of the pithy comment, he was once asked by Joe Craig if one of his machines vibrated much. "The only problem," replied Harold, "Is that when I wipe my goggles I don't know which handlebar to put my hand on."

1950 SENIOR TT. After finishing second in the Junior race, Geoff dominated the Senior race. Fuel was now 80 octane, and he made full use of the extra power and the Featherbed's handling to lift the race record to 92.27mph – higher than Harold Daniell's 12-years-old lap record – and left the lap record at 93.33mph. Artie Bell was second, Johnny Lockett third and Harold Daniell fifth; only reigning World Champion Les Graham managing to divide the victorious Norton squad.

One of the supreme stylists of all time, this is Geoff Duke at Kate's Cottage during that 93.33mph lap. One-piece leathers were a revolution he introduced, after realising that the bulky two-piece style that was normal was affecting his top speed.

1951 PROTOTYPE. During 1951, a prototype was built using an adaption of the Featherbed frame with a semi-monocoque rear end and powered by a 500cc Dominator engine. The headlamp cowling and built-in front number plate were an attempt to bring the styling up to the standard of tidy front ends set by Triumph's successful nacelle arrangement. A deeply valanced mudguard completed the effect.

1951 PROTOTYPE. The rear end continued the theme of comprehensive protection from road dirt for the rider, and beneath the side-hinged seat were the toolbox and access to the oil tank filler. Silencer shape was very similar to that on the Dominator 88 shown for the first time at the Earls Court show at the end of the year. Perhaps it was too revolutionary and Norton knew their conservative market well, for it did not get into production.

HOPWOOD TWIN. Bert Hopwood's design for a Norton twin was destined to live on after the Bracebridge Street works was closed, and proved capable of being stretched in capacity far beyond what the original drawing had envisaged.

It was unusual in using a single camshaft, across the front of the crankcase and operating substantial cam followers that effectively limited the revs to 6500. A three-piece crank featured a cast iron flywheel 7 inches in diameter and 1.875 inches wide with the manganese molybdenum crank halves bolted to it. Connecting rods were of RR56 alloy, with separate shell bearings. Main bearings were roller on the drive side and ball on the timing side.

The splayed exhaust ports gave a good flow of air between them and the very early engine had the inlet manifold cast in the iron head, changed to separate ports with a detachable manifold early in the life of the series. The flat-topped pistons had distinct left or right hand cylinder valve cutaways, and when the author was working in a London dealer's service department the results of misassembly and subsequent high revs by unskilled owners were seen to be quite expensive!

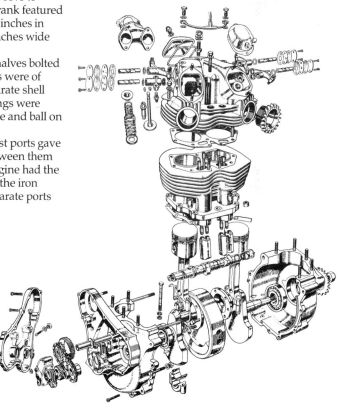

1951 SEASON. For the 1951 season, Duke had the developed works machines with neater rear suspension units and revised engines, the 350 now 75.9 x 77mm and the 500 84 x 90mm. He responded with a Junior/Senior double in the TT, leaving the absolute lap record at 95.22mph, and went on to win four other rounds of the 350 World Championship series and two of the 500, achieving the first ever 350/500 double World Championship.

WAC McCANDLESS. The McCandless family talent was not confined to designing and building machines that set new standards. WAC "Cromie" McCandless was a very able rider, with a win in the 1949 350cc Manx Grand Prix to his credit, mounted then on a Francis Beart-prepared Manx. In 1951 Cromie rode a works machine to third place in the Senior TT, to round off a week that saw his only TT win, taking an Italian FB Mondial to victory in the very first 125cc race in the Isle of Man series.

As well as his regular rides on the Beart Nortons, Cromie was given a one-off ride on a works Gilera-4 in the 1952 Ulster Grand Prix and showed his ability to pace himself by outlasting the bigger names to win.

1951 JUNIOR TT. Johnny Lockett's best TT result was second place to Duke in the 1951 Junior race, with Jack Brett making it a Norton 1-2-3; here he approaches Hillberry during his fine 1951 ride. Johnny was a useful trials rider too, capable of winning first-class awards in National events, such as the 1951 Cotswold, when he lost no marks but was beaten in the special tests.

ERIC OLIVER. The great Eric Oliver in full flight at Silverstone during the 1951 BMCRC Hutchinson 100 meeting, when he and passenger Enrico Dobelli won the Mellano Trophy. This was the first Featherbed frame to race with a sidecar – a Watsonian – and used the leading-axle fork with large diameter hollow front wheel spindle that had first been seen on the works solo machines in 1949 and was adopted by Oliver from 1951 until 1954.

DON SLATE. During the early 1950s, sidecar racing was in the throes of a great change, with some outfits still usable on both grass and tarmac racing tracks, and others becoming specially adapted to one particular field of competition.

Don Slate, seen here on his 596cc single overhead camshaft Manx outfit, was a force to be reckoned with wherever he rode. A leading grass track competitor, he would also enter for a Brands Hatch road race meeting and show how a rather scruffy outfit could go. In one special Challenge Match at Brands, he beat Jack Surtees' 1000cc Vincent outfit and on another occasion stayed ahead of Cyril Smith's very quick 500cc outfit.

Slate's machine dated from the 1930s and no doubt the fact that "dope" fuel was permitted was a great aid to performance. There is still at least one element of the War evident in the crew's dress, since they are both wearing ex-Don R boots, with laces.

PIP HARRIS. "Pip" Harris was always noted for an outfit that was both smart and quick. Here, in 1951, he forces his 596cc single ohc, dating from the middle 1930s, to another victory as passenger Clements carries on the usual fight with centrifugal force.

The sidecar is the standard raceware of almost all leading men at the time, a Watsonian, which could be supplied to fit rigid or spring frames, the factory carrying out any tailoring to fit, if necessary. Of interest is the completely exposed primary chain, affording no protection for either driver or passenger; lubrication to the top run of the chain is by an adjustable gravity feed from the base of the oil tank.

"Pip", the son of an ex-TT rider, raced Nortons for many years, with only a brief break to wrestle with the Vincent factory's "Gunga Din" V-twin for a season in the 1000cc class, before succumbing to the German onslaught on the sidecar class and going over to BMW power.

1952 ISDT. The factory prepared three Featherbed-framed 500cc twins for the 1951 ISDT in Italy, and Rex Young, Dick Clayton and Jack Breffitt all rode the six days without penalty to bring back a Manufacturer's Team Prize.

In 1952 Rex Young was nursing injuries from a road accident and his mount was taken over by Worcester clubman HL 'Don' Williams, who took time off from the business started by his TT-winning father Eric (1914 and '21 Juniors) to ride through the rain and snow of September in Austria to win a Gold Medal for losing no marks. The dented exhaust system tells more about the event than mere words.

1952 CLAYTON TRIAL. At the 1952 Clayton Trial, Bob Collier of the Experimental Department (left) was competing in the sidecar class with passenger Gordon Wilde (right). They kept a helpful eye on Australian visitor Harry "Chisel" Hinton, who was a leading road racer of the period and so nicknamed because he was considered very sharp – enough for it not to be common knowledge that he had a glass eye. Second from the right is Bill Young, an Australian Norton agent who visited the factory to learn about their servicing methods and was a good trials rider, winning the Cambrian Cup during his visit.

DAVE BENNETT. Dave Bennett won the 1951 Senior Manx Grand Prix and was a member of the works team for the 1952 season. His first International Grand Prix was the Swiss, and when team leader Duke retired he took on the AJS team in a battle for the lead, but crashed fatally on the penultimate lap at the Tenni corner. A member of the Kings Norton MCC, he had graduated to road racing from the Ariel competition shop.

ALL-ROUNDER DUKE. Duke's talents spread beyond solos, and in the 1952 D K Mansell Trial he borrowed Bob Collier's sidecar outfit and passenger Ian Leaf to win an award with 14 marks lost. He was an accomplished scrambler, too, riding as a member of the British team in the 1948 Moto Cross des Nations. His road racing career was so outstanding that his ranking as an all-rounder is frequently overlooked.

SONS OF CRAIG. It was all unofficial and if Joe Craig knew about it, he never let on. But both his sons raced, and it wasn't discussed in front of him at the factory. Reg, the younger of the two, had a few outings like this one at Brands Hatch, but Des became proficient enough to be entered by Comerfords of Thames Ditton, for whom he worked at one time. Both the Craig brothers spoke with a strong Ulster accent, acquired from their father, although Reg had never been there.

POP SWINNERTON. Rem Fowler never lost touch with the Norton factory and was always made welcome there as the man who brought them the very first of so many TT victories. He is on the left here, swapping notes with the renowned "Pop" Swinnerton, who joined the company as a lad during the 1914-18 War and became part of the legend.

"Pop" was once given notice during the early 1950s when times were not good and staff cuts had to be made. Notice or not, "Pop" was back at his bench on Monday, timing the ignition of each engine, as he had done for years. When forman Bill Stone reminded him that he had been dismissed, "Pop" simply told Bill that not even Managing Director Gilbert Smith could get rid of him.

With the entire staff of the Engine Department looking down from their gallery workplaces, Bill Stone fetched Gilbert Smith to tell "Pop" that he was no longer an employee. Smith, according to those who witnessed the incident, saw what the source of the problem was and turned to Bill Stone, saying: "I can't sack him. He's been here longer than me." To cheers from the gallery, Smith and Stone returned to their respective offices and "Pop" Swinnerton carried on timing the magnetos, as he had done for so many years.

NORTON SIDECAR. The factory were still offering Norton sidecars in 1952, although the range was limited to the Model G single seater at £83.12.0d. But they still displayed their name to spectators at racing events, as a reminder that they had machines in the range specifically intended as sidecar models. In September of that year Pip Harris carried the name on his Manx outfit, while Eric Oliver with the works engine in his frame carried the Watsonian name.

1953 INTERNATIONAL. For 1953 the International was available in Featherbed form, the announcement coming two months after the basic range was detailed in the press. With BSA's Gold Star models winning both Clubman's races at the TT, something was needed to give the Inter a new lease of life. The new models came with alloy barrel and head with cast iron valve seats. "Should prove pre-eminent in the high-speed touring class," said *Motor Cycling* in its review.

The revised gearbox with horizontal end cover was standard and also an 8 inch front brake with each shoe on a separate fulcrum pin. The list of extras was impressive: folding kickstart, racing footrest and gearlever, racing mudguards, straight-through exhaust and even a flyscreen could be ordered. Norton wanted the Clubman's TT back in their camp and Bob Keeler rewarded them in the 1953 Senior event. But thereafter the Gold Stars reigned and the Inter quietly faded away, its last mention in the range for the 1958 season listing the 500 at £303.2.10d.

RAY AMM. Geoff Duke left Norton at the end of 1952 to join the Gilera team, having added the 350 World Championship to his tally but recognising the potential of the Italian machines. His place was taken by Rhodesian Ray Amm, who had been recruited during 1952 when injury put Duke out of action.

Ray faced the challenge from Duke's Gilera and Les Graham's much improved MV at the Senior TT, having already won the Junior race. Duke fell at Quarter Bridge when chasing Amm and Les Graham died tragically at the bottom of Bray Hill; Amm set the lap record at 97.41mph and went on to win the race. As he tackles the decent of Bray Hill in tigerish manner, he tucks himself away behind the tiny flyscreen. The small tank above the primary chain guard is the container for the chain oiler.

1953 JUNIOR TT. Ray Amm tells Joe Craig how he guided the Norton to another win after his victory in the 1953 Junior race while his wife and mother look pensive. Ken Kavanagh (49) was second and Jack Brett (41) fourth to take the Manufacturer's Team Prize. Amm was a deeply religious man – how Pa Norton would have approved of him – and would pray before each race. For 1953 the works machines featured oil-cooled exhaust valves and during practice Amm tried the experimental kneeler that was banned by the TT scrutineers.

500T IN ITS ELEMENT. Same man, same machine, different sport. Fred Lewis also rode his trials 500T in scrambles, just as most private owners would do before the different branches of the sport became so diversified as to make it impracticable. The 500T's tank was shaped to give a slim grip for the knees and was mounted on horizontal rubber prongs at the front with a single retaining bolt at the rear. Compression ratio was slightly down on the equivalent roadster ES2 engine, 6:1 compared with 6:16:1, and wide ratio gears gave overall ratios of 18.2, 13.1, 8.1 and 5.5:1. The 500T was dropped from the range at the end of 1954.

500T. The 500T was a popular mount with club riders, although the 350T introduced in 1951 never caught on. The works riders were right up at the head of the league, Rex Young finishing second in the ACU Trials Drivers' Star competition in both 1950 and '51. The 500T had outstanding low-speed pulling, here being used by Worcester Auto Club member Fred Lewis in the 1953 Welsh Two Day Trial. Fred was an outstanding local notary, and was later to become the Lord Mayor of the City of Worcester.

JOHN SURTEES. John Surtees at Thruxton in 1953, riding his 350 Manx to another win. John was unique in making his mark as a young man on a 500cc Vincent Grey Flash instead of the more usual Norton. He was quite an embarrassment to Nortons in his formative years, harrying the works machines on short circuits and once lapping Ray Amm during a 25-lap race at Brands Hatch – before Amm became a works rider.

This talent was too good to miss and Joe Craig signed him up for the works team in 1954, in support of Ray Amm and Ken Kavanagh. But that was the year the might of Italy took over, Amm finishing second to Anderson (Guzzi) in the 350 World title and to Duke (Gilera) in the 500, so John did not shine internationally. In 1955 he rode a development of the production Manx, as AMC policy dictated, and was fourth in the Junior TT. He ended the season at Silverstone beating Geoff Duke's Gilera in a race that made a fitting swansong for Joe Craig.

See these NEW models on stand 134

DOMINATOR DE-LUXE MODEL 88

DOMINATOR MODEL 7

MODEL ES2

MODEL 19R

Norton The World's Best Road Holders

NORTON MOTORS LTD · BRACEBRIDGE ST · BIRMINGHAM 6

1954 RANGE. The 1954 range showed a wide range of performance and equipment levels, the 19R, with its 82 x 113mm bore and stroke, dating back to 1933 and retaining the rigid frame for the few traditional sidecar drivers; the 19S was identical apart from the swinging fork rear suspension which added 5lb to the 367lb dry weight of the rigid model. The adoption of the new roundel tank badge identified the year of manufacture, but did nothing to hide the Model 19's long-standing origins. The rigid version was phased out at the end of 1955 and the springer in 1958.

The ES2 retained the 79 x 100mm measurements that recalled the days when it was arguably the finest sports machine the public could buy. But its Brooklands heritage was a memory only for the older enthusiast and twins were the vogue. It still found a small but steady sale until its demise some years later.

The Dominator Model 7's place in the range must have puzzled many, since it had been overshadowed by the Featherbed-framed Dominator 88 since the latter's announcement. But frame stocks had to be used up, and the factory were very definite in their statements that a sidecar could

not be fitted to the Featherbed frame – even though some did it as a private effort and gladly sacrificed any question of a factory guarantee in the event of failure. The Model 88 was the most desirable machine in the range for 1955, its racing pedigree combining with a twin-cylinder engine that was proving reliable and as fast as the majority of the opposition. The Dominator was a pointer to the way forward for Norton, making the most of their remarkable racing record to sell sporting high-performance machines in a world that was becoming more affluent and looking for more than mundane transport.

1954 16H. The 16H lasted as a catalogue model until 1954, its 79 x 100mm side valve engine the only difference from its bigger brother, the Big 4, which still had the 82 x 113mm engine. The 16H was geared for solo work with a

5:1 top gear, though it cannot have been sold to many to be used in that form. The Big 4 was listed as "normally geared for sidecar work" at 5.6:1 and did not have the separate lower lens for the parking light that was the

norm for the 1954 range. Both models came with sidecar lugs as standard, visible here beneath saddle and tank nose. Both models were dropped by 1955 and a tangible link with James Norton was lost.

1955 DOMINATOR 88. The Dominator 88 was first shown at the 1951 Earls Court Show as an export only model, as Reynold Tubes could only supply limited quantities of the Featherbed frame and the Bracebridge Street factory was not able to make them. It came on to the home market in 1952, with the plunger-frame Model 7 also available and priced £27 lower at £239.

For 1955 the traditional Norton tank lettering was changed to the screwed-on plate seen on this example, and the deeply valanced mudguard of the early models had been replaced by a slimmer, more sporting style. Instruments were mounted in a panel on the fork top yoke and the shorter tank gave a rather untidy glimpse of the steering head.

19R. A rare bird was the 19R, made for the 1954 and 1955 seasons to use up the old rigid frame stocks; it was not even listed in the factory's abridged catalogue for 1954. It naturally came with sidecar lugs, an end use to which the 82 x 113mm engine was best suited, the low-revving unit giving 25bhp at 4200rpm. The engine continued in the swinging-fork frame as the 19S until 1958.

When the AMC-designed gearbox was introduced in 1956, it had been tested in a 19S sidecar outfit loaded with 300lb over 20,000 miles and gave no problems. It then did 10,000 miles in a Dominator 99, again without fault, before it was accepted as suitable for the range.

1955 MODEL 7. The Model 7 for 1955 still used the swinging-fork frame rushed into production for the 1953 season to meet the demand for that style of suspension that had embarrassed the factory when the Featherbed roadsters were first introduced. The brazed frame came complete with sidecar lugs and the model's weight penalty of 420lb against the Model 88's 393lb made it clear that this was to be regarded as touring machine. It was made until 1956, when it was fitted with the 600cc engine and renamed the Model 77, intended as a luxury sidecar machine.

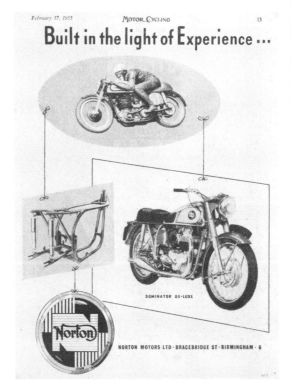

February 17, 1955   MOTOR CYCLING   13

Built in the light of Experience ...

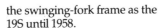

DOMINATOR DE-LUXE

Norton

NORTON MOTORS LTD · BRACEBRIDGE ST · BIRMINGHAM · 6

1953 MANX. Another angle on the Dominator for 1955, its relation to the success of the works racers emphasised by the picture of Ray Amm, second in both 350 and 500cc World Championships the year before, including another Senior TT win. But the picture is actually of his 1953 Senior mount – for 1954 the works motors had an outside flywheel.

DESPATCH RIDER. Joe Craig's sons Reg and Desmond worked at Bracebridge Street, Reg being a member of the road test crew. Combining the matter of test mileage with the job of despatch riding in the mid 1950s brought both income and publicity as the company's riders co-operated with the *Evening Despatch* to ferry urgent films and copy around the country, with development miles being added at the same time. Here is Reg Craig, looking suitably relieved at getting the weight of the despatch sack off his back and safely delivered to its London destination. The lugged-frame ES2 of 1955 looks road-soiled without appearing scruffy.

JOE CRAIG RETIRES. At the end of 1955, an era closed with Joe Craig's retirement. No man could have filled his position as the head of such a successful racing team without incurring criticism and jealousy, but no-one could deny his talent for developing a basically old engine design and for spotting young racing talent. His development team presented him with the customary tankard and a mounted Manx conrod as a farewell memento against a background of a works Manx. Left to right are Ivor Smith (test bench), Harry Salter (machinist), Arthur Edwards (mechanic), Bill Clark (cylinder head specialist), Frank Sharratt (engine builder) and one unidentified onlooker.

MODEL 99. From late 1955 the Featherbed Dominator theme was extended with the introduction of the Model 99. The 68 x 82mm engine developed 31bhp at 5750rpm on a compression ratio of 7.4:1 and was an easier high-speed cruiser with its top gear of 4.53:1 compared with the 88's 5:1, thanks to a 21-tooth engine sprocket on the bigger machine.

1957 SENIOR TT. 1957 racing policy was to lend developments of the production Manx models to dealer-entrants, and Reg Dearden's choice of rider was Alan Trow, while Eric Houseley of Chapel-en-le-Frith entered local lad John Hartle and Lord Montagu of Beaulieu backed Jack Brett. That year's eight-lap Senior TT was dominated by Bob McIntyre with the first 100mph lap on the works Gilera 4 and the best all-British finisher was Trow on Dearden's Manx, seen here during a running-in session at Brands Hatch.

JOE CRAIG KILLED. Craig went to live in Holland after leaving Bracebridge Street, marrying Nelly Wijngarten in 1956. In 1957 the couple were retracing their honeymoon route of the previous year and had a car accident at Innsbruck, Joe was killed. At the inquest he was reported to have suffered a heart attack, whether as a result of the accident or the cause of it was not known. A four-times winner of the 600cc class in the Ulster Grand Prix in the 1920s and a works rider before taking over as team manager, he had been the architect of Norton's outstanding periods of racing success in two quite separate eras.

As the Norton factory approached the 60th anniversary of its founding, it was facing growing competition on both touring and racing fronts. Its ambitions in racing had been curbed by the financial problems of 1952 and later by the strictures of its new owners. A policy of "race what you make" would not win Grands Prix against the Italians with 4 and 8 cylinder machines, and the Manx continued as a mount for the private owner, not a design to beat the world in 1957.

The roadster range had been trimmed of the slow selling 500T trials machine and the gentle but unexciting 16H and Big 4 side-valves. The world was demanding performance and that meant more cylinders and more ccs than the old designs could reliably offer. The Dominator in its 600cc form was a sports tourer to match almost anything the competition could offer and could be the basis of new models for growing foreign markets. Bracebridge Street had a lot to offer, but its hands were tied by the policies of the parent company.

But there had been some remarkable innovations from this company, which some regarded as old fashioned, both from its own personnel and from those connected with it. They are worth a final look.

Experiments and Novelties

While the works racing team struggled gamely with their single cylinder models in the face of growing four cylinder opposition from the Italian Gilera and MV factories, there was a great deal of experimental work going on both in and outside the factory.

There had been a little known programme with a water-cooled Manx in the Experimental Shop at Bracebridge Street, but it did not race. The Featherbed, although it was a major step forward in the basic matter of roadholding, was not the end of the line so far as competition was concerned; there followed the remarkable "kneeler" that appeared on a few occasions. There was the F type racing model too, with a horizontal development of the established Manx engine built in unit with the gearbox. And there was an exciting four cylinder model that was shelved after the new owners, Associated Motor Cycles, dictated a policy of the group using only developments of over-the-counter racing models. With that decision some revolutionary designs were killed off and

the Italians were left to dominate international racing, although the private owners chased them hard with their own adaptations of the standard Manx.

In the sidecar class there was innovation, too. Much of it came from the fertile brain of Eric Oliver, who was able to build whatever the regulations would allow in this thirst for success. In trials, Bob Collier was not bound by any restrictive policy and brought success to the company name by adapting basic models to suit the sidecar class of that most individual of sports, as did Arthur Humphries with his International hitched to a sidecar.

International motocross saw Norton success, too, with Les Archer making his mark on a special Dominator-powered model before changing to an overhead camshaft single and gaining even more victories. The very racing success of the factory over many years made them the obvious choice as the basis of experiments by innovators in many fields.

SIDECAR CHAMPION. Eric Oliver's brave riding was a major factor in his winning the World Sidecar Championship four times in its first five years of existence. He was also an innovator and his adoption of the Featherbed frame with a leading axle telescopic fork was the first of many changes he made to the established order of three-wheeled racing. He won three of the five rounds in the 1951 World series, including the Belgian Grand Prix, which he is here leading from his great rival, Ercole Frigerio, on the Gilera 4. The races in the 1951 title chase that Eric did not win went to Gilera pilots, one each to Frigerio and Albino Milani.

CYRIL SMITH. Oliver broke his leg in a minor event early in the 1952 season and it seemed the World Championship was to be left to the Gilera entries. Cyril Smith, ex-chief road tester at Norton, had other ideas. The first race in the series was the Swiss, and Cyril finished five seconds behind Milani's Italian four, having led at half distance. His reward was the use of a "Joe's motor" for the season and the tough little Birmingham pipe-smoker used it to good effect through the season, clinching the title at the final round when Ernesto Merlo's Gilera succumbed to magneto trouble while Smith and passenger Les Nutt kept going, despite struggling with a fractured front down tube, to finish third.

Smith's winning outfit was unusual in 1952. While others had followed Eric Oliver's move to rear suspension, he had a special rigid back end built onto the Featherbed. It did not seem to slow him during the Berlin meeting where he is seen here, lapping at over 90mph despite the indifferent-looking surface.

NORTON FOUR. The Norton "Four" occupied Joe Craig's time during the late 1940s, when he spent a lot of time with the BRM factory in Lincolnshire. But the new lease of life that the Featherbed frame gave to the single cylinder engine was enough to delay the idea, if not kill it. And the financial troubles of 1952 combined with the later restrictions imposed by AMC made certain it was not revived.

Water-cooled and intended to be mounted transversely, it was in unit with the gearbox, driving by gear inboard of the timing side main bearing. Double overhead camshafts were driven by a train of gears and opened the valves via slipper-type cam followers; hairpin valve springs then closed them.

The cylinders had wet liners that screwed into the head and were sealed at the base by rubber rings; the exhaust valve guides were finned to give a greater area exposed to the cooling water. A slave 125cc single-cylinder unit was built and bench tested, but the Norton Four got no further.

PROTOTYPE 500 TWIN. A prototype rigid-framed 500 twin was built for tests prior to the 1950 International Six Days Trial, Bob Collier fitting a Model 7 engine into a 500T frame for evaluation purposes. Not used by the factory team, who opted on that occasion for the established plunger sprung frame, it was used to some effect by Collier in one-day trials later.

He first rode it with a factory trade plate fitted, and was hauled over the coals when the Joe Craig saw the picture of a trade plate in competition. Bob Collier had used a black tank initially, but the colour had to be altered to the established Norton silver and black before he was allowed to register the machine properly and

ride it with the management's blessing. This he did well enough to win the sidecar class of both the Cotswold Cup and the Red Rose Trial in 1953.

Here Bob and regular passenger Gordon Wilde concentrate on the rocks ahead as they steer their way to victory in the Cotswold. The team of Collier and Wilde became known for their daredevil tactics with this and subsequent twins, having to build up sufficient speed before entering the section for sheer impetus to help them through, the lack of slogging traction making the twin something of an "all-or-nothing" machine. Bob's description of their tactics was "Start three fields back and let it rip."

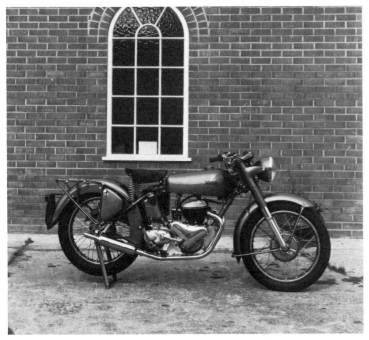

MILITARY PROTOTYPE. The old 16H was replaced by Triumph's TRW side-valve twin in the early 1950s and the loss of the military business left a gap in production. Bill Pitcher drew up a rival to the Triumph, using the established bottom end of the Dominator twin and adding a side-valve layout, allowing access to the tappets via a small cover at the front of the cylinder block. Mounted on the crankshaft was an alternator, itself inside a cast alloy primary chaincase – quite a breakaway for a traditional company.

Mounted in a shortened 16H frame with Roadholder forks, it was liked by the Army testers, but the Triumph was established and another model on the strength would have doubled the spending on spares. Good though the Norton might have been, it couldn't persuade the Army to stretch the budget and remained a one-off.

The sole example is now owned by Sammy Miller, in whose museum it now lives, painted in civilian colours.

1953 KNEELER. During practice for the 1953 TT, Ray Amm rode the revolutionary kneeler that was to be known variously as "The Amm Sandwich" or "The Silver Fish". It was a searching test for a new concept in works Nortons, designed by the McCandlesses from the beginning to be a streamliner, with the weight of

the fuel carried low in pannier tanks. It had been raced once, in the North West 200, but retired with engine bothers.

But it didn't start in the Junior TT, the team having been told by the scrutineers that they wouldn't pass it for racing, whatever Ray Amm might think of it.

KNEELER FRAME. The kneeler frame was based on the Featherbed's bottom cradle, but the top tubes were splayed around the engine and down to the back of the gearbox. Comprehensive padding protected Amm's abdomen and knees and, in the manner of a true kneeler, there were no footrests.

Fuel was lifted from the shaped fuel tanks to a weir-type carburettor by a pump driven off the end of the inlet camshaft. After one more practice session, at the Dutch TT, Amm went back to the normal Featherbed model and finished third in the World Championship in the 350 class.

MONTLHÉRY RECORDS. The kneeler did get in the record books before the 1953 season ended. On November 8th and 9th that year it was ridden around the Montlhéry banked circuit by Eric Oliver and Ray Amm to break a total of 61 world speed records. 350 and 500cc engines were used, running on methyl alcohol, and a small header tank between the pump and the carburettor overcame earlier problems with flooding.

The 350 engine took records up to 1000cc for durations up to seven hours, for which period it averaged 120.15mph. The 500 engine took records up to one hour, which included 750 and 1000cc class figures as well, and recorded one lap at an average of 145.4mph. The absolute track record at the time was held by a supercharged 3-litre Alfa Romeo at 147.86mph.

Joe Craig watches intently as Amm gets back aboard for another run. The machine was run without the rear fairing, to make tyre changes easier and to keep the Avon cool.

1954 BEMROSE TRIAL. The Collier/Wilde team in action again, this time tackling Hollinsclough in the 1954 Bemrose Trial, with the familiar figure of Ralph Venables watching from the left.

The front forks seen here were a product of Bob Collier's fertile mind, using standard stanchions and steel fabricated bottom legs and trailing links that combined with standard Girling dampers to give a greatly improved action. The idea was subsequently tried on the works racers, but the official version of Bob Collier's homespun experiment had altered the trail and made no provision for fine adjustment of the damping. It was not successful during initial tests at the Motor Industry's Association track at Nuneaton, nor later when tried in anger at a minor Belgian meeting. The official factory racing machines stayed true to the established Roadholder telescopic forks for the season.

61 RECORDS. A happy gathering on November 9th, with 61 world's records in the bag! Left to right are Alan Wilson (competitions manager), Joe Craig, Eric Oliver, Bill Clark (engine builder) and Ray Amm. Mechanic Arthur Edwards is in the grimy overalls to the right.

Despite this proof of its high-speed stability (it ran on ribbed Avon tyres front and rear) the kneeler was not used again in this form. But Eric Oliver had realised how effective the lower centre of gravity could be in a sidecar outfit.

KNEELER OUTFIT. Eric Oliver's fully-faired kneeler for the 1954 season established the kneeler style of outfit, and the line runs on to the present day. It was his final push for the World Championship, but Noll's BMW set another trend that was to last a long time by winning the title, and Eric had to accept second place. At the Belgian Grand Prix that year, however, he set a new lap record at 95.4mph as he beat Noll, and is seen here exiting from La Source hairpin, with passenger Les Nutt almost hidden.

LES ARCHER. Les Archer was one of the famous Aldershot family of racing men, but the road racing game was not for him. Instead, he developed a 490cc Manx engine in a frame that was a blend of Featherbed and single top tube, with single leading shoe Manx conical hubs, into a scrambler that was a regular winner at home and in the tough moto-cross events on the Continent. In 1956 the European Championship was introduced, the series that was eventually to become the World Championship. In a frantic season of racing, servicing and driving across Europe, Les Archer took the European title in its inaugural year.

BOB McINTYRE. Keeping a privately-entered Manx Norton up with the "foreign menace" was a task that demanded a machine prepared to an exceptional standard and a rider of outstanding ability. The great Bob McIntyre was certainly a great rider and, with sponsor Joe Potts' tuning skills to speed him on his way, he didn't give up the struggle. In 1955, his Manx Norton wearing the full streamlining that factory policy would not let the works entries use, he rode his heart out in the Junior TT to split the Moto-Guzzi pair of Bill Lomas and Cecil Sandford and take second place. All eyes are on Bob Mac as he exits Braddan Bridge, the Mercury MCC badge decorating his helmet.

TRIALS SPECIAL. John Catchpole rode some of the most ingenious specials the trials world had ever seen, in both solo and sidecar form. One of his notable sidecar outfits was powered by an alloy-head 16H engine, driving through the old Sturmey Archer style of gearbox that had withstood the boots of many thousands of Dispatch Riders during active service.

Here John uses the pulling power of the faithful old side valve as he fights for grip in the Hoad Trophies Trial. It was a brave effort, using such an historic design to complete with more modern machines, but John did not bring glory to the Bracebridge Street name on this occasion.

Sixty Years Old

In February 1958 Gilbert Smith left the Norton company he had joined in 1916; his service contract was not renewed by the AMC group. On his last day at the factory he told George Rowley, the Midlands Buyer for Norton, Shelley, James and Francis Barnett, that the old faces did not fit any longer. He retired to his home in Tanworth-in-Arden, saying he would take a rest before looking for another position, but died without joining another company at the age of 62.

The 1958 range consolidated what had been established, although this was the final year the name "International" appeared in the price list. Pushrod singles of 350, 500 and 600cc capacities were offered, and the lugged frame with a twin cylinder engine lived on briefly in the Model 77, a 600cc sidecar model. The Featherbed Dominator 88 and 99 were offered with alternators as the highspots of the range and, for many, the last of the real Nortons.

MODEL **E.S.2.**

500 c.c. SINGLE

Latest in a long line of illustrious 500 c.c. O.H.V. machines, combining reasonably high maximum performance with low speed tractability and economy.
Unapproachable for continued regular service with minimum maintenance, there's an attractive air of restrained urgency about its black and chrome finish.

Over 95,000,000 miles in 10 years !
Reliability exemplified by R.A.C. Patrolmen.

BUILT IN THE LIGHT OF EXPERIENCE

1958 ES2. The ES2 in the brazed lugged frame with swinging fork rear end died in 1958, still made in the traditional silver and black that recalled the history of the model. It was the end of the 79 x 100mm line that had started in the days of James Norton and in its final year was priced at £242.12.9d. It was still standard wear with the R.A.C. patrol sidecar outfits and the claim of 95,000,000 miles in 10 years confirmed the service it had given to thousands of owners over the years.

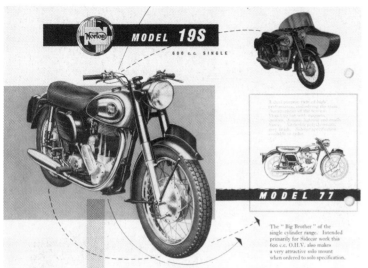

1958 19S. The 19S was a simple model that could trace its ancestors back to the 1920s, with its 82 x 113mm pushrod engine thoroughly outdated by the time the line ended in 1958. "Intended primarily for sidecar work," said the company's literature, as the small car made ready to take over as the accepted family transport. At £254.9.10d it offered old fashioned value for money in a world that wanted something better.

1958 DOMINATOR 99. Fast, recognised as the machine by which others judged their handling, and one of the best looking motorcycles to leave a British factory, the 100mph 600cc Dominator 99 is a high note on which to close this story of the Norton motorcycle from 1898 to 1958. A proud machine to carry the name that had started so modestly all those years ago, yet which made its mark upon the world.

General Index

Model Index